MALLARDS AND THE MOURNE MOUNTAINS *Oil Painting 18″ × 15″*

WILD CHORUS

WRITTEN AND ILLUSTRATED BY

PETER SCOTT

LONDON: COUNTRY LIFE LIMITED
2-10 TAVISTOCK STREET, COVENT GARDEN, W.C.2
NEW YORK: CHARLES SCRIBNER'S SONS

SIGNED LIMITED EDITION, NOVEMBER 1938
FIRST ORDINARY EDITION, SEPTEMBER 1939
REPRINTED NOVEMBER 1939
REPRINTED APRIL 1941
REPRINTED SEPTEMBER 1942
REPRINTED MAY 1944
REPRINTED APRIL 1946
REPRINTED APRIL 1947
REPRINTED DECEMBER 1948
REPRINTED 1949

PRINTED AND MADE IN GREAT BRITAIN BY ROBERT MACLEHOSE AND CO. LTD. THE UNIVERSITY PRESS, GLASGOW

CONTENTS

PLATES IN SEPIA

of tails, the curve of necks, and all the details of movement which make a bird in flight one of nature's most perfect expressions.

But, although it is thrilling to be able to see all these birds at close quarters, the true setting for wild geese is far from even the loneliest human habitation, out on the wild marshes and mudflats where they roost at night and whence they flight in to feed at dawn, silhouetted against the eastern sky.

MID-ISLAND STRANGFORD LOUGH AND THE BRENTS

Oil Painting 55″ × 33″

CHAPTER ONE

THE CHORUS OF THE GEESE

IN the crazy world of today, when the human race seems so little able to control its destiny, when crises and depressions follow each other in mad succession, the need for escape is more urgent and the call of wild places more insistent than ever.

In England few of these wild places are left. For some there are forests and fells and moors, for others the ocean, but, for me, wildest of all are the saltings and mudflats of the coast. Here the sky is master of the scene; the grandeur of sunrise and sunset is reflected in the tidal pools and, dully, on the surface of the wet mud. The creeks wind sluggishly from the marshes towards the open sea, and at flood tide the sea itself comes wandering back. At spring tides it whispers through the grass and washes against the sea walls. In this world live the wildfowl, and in this same flat world I like to live, within sight of their winter hordes and within sound of their wild chorus.

They are mysterious birds coming from far-away northern lands, impelled by an unknown force and kept infallibly on their course by an unknown sense. They are wild and wary birds, a traditional quarry of man from immemorial times. Their flight is swift and their formations fill the sky, but I believe that their greatest appeal is to the ear. When the north-east wind blows at dawn, and the flood tide creeps in across the mud, it is the sudden call of geese, half heard above the roar of wind and waves, that brings the greatest thrill of all. When the full moon rises over the marsh at dusk, and the creeks are brimful; when eyes are strained to see which way the bubbles float, so that one may know if full-sea is past or yet to come, it is the call of geese which makes one's heart leap.

THE CHORUS OF THE GEESE

The wigeon whistle as they come swishing low along the edge of the marsh; the mallards chuckle to themselves as they go inland high up in the sunset sky; the curlews call as they flight from the incoming tide and the redshanks pipe in their creeks. These are the familiar sounds of the saltings in winter, but the music of the geese is the most stirring of all.

Whether they are pink-feet in East Anglia, greylags in Westmorland, barnacles in Scotland, brents in Ireland, whitefronts in Hungary, lesser whitefronts in Persia, or snow geese in Canada, and widely different as the calls of the various species are, the music of the great skeins is always moving in its grandeur, always perfectly appropriate to the wild places in which it is heard.

By the musician the works of a composer may perhaps be judged after the first hearing, but for me the full enjoyment of a symphony does not come until I am familiar with it. So it is with the chorus of the geese. The familiar high note of the pink-foot remains my favourite wild goose call, the note that I have heard across the moonlit potato fields, across the saltings of my home, and out over the bare mudflats in the dawn.

LA TOILETTE. PINKFOOTED GEESE *Oil Painting 30″ × 25″*

CHAPTER TWO

ANABEL

I suppose the return of Anabel on that October morning was one of the half dozen most stirring events that I have ever experienced. The thrill was no less because it was half expected. I had never really doubted that she would come back, but when she did I was overwhelmed with joy and relief and wonder.

Anabel is a pink-footed goose. On September 25th, 1936, she came first to the lighthouse which is my home. It was early in the season and the winter flocks of geese which live on the near-by marshes had not yet arrived. Soon after sunrise Anabel, led by that strange instinct which enables young birds to precede the old ones on the southward migration, came to the salt-marshes of the Wash. She heard some geese calling below her and swung in towards them. There were twenty-nine of them, sitting on the marsh quite near a strange round building; but they did not seem to be alarmed by it, so Anabel swept round low over them and called in answer and immediately a great babel arose. Anabel was very pleased to find others of her kind, and she circled round again. She did not realise that they were tame pink-feet which had lived several years at the lighthouse. As she passed a little plantation some rooks came out and mobbed her; but she was too tired to care, so she curled back with set wings and settled near the pinioned geese on the marsh. They didn't greet her in a very friendly way, considering that she was one of their own kind. Some of the more pugnacious ganders chased and pecked her, but Anabel was too tired to run away and so she just crouched down and waited till they had satisfied their anger. Then she stood up again, preened herself, flapped her wings and walked after the other geese towards a fresh water pool, which is just above high tide mark on the side of the sea wall.

On her way to the pool she walked past me, as I stood watching from the top of the bank in my bright blue dressing gown (for it was not yet breakfast time), and she showed no fear, although she passed no more than twenty yards from me; indeed she gave me the most casual glance, although I was possibly the first human being she had ever seen. From her plumage I knew that she could only be at most three months old, and it was clear that, in her manner towards human beings, she thought it wise to follow the lead of her elders and betters. Since they showed no undue alarm, why should she?

A week later Anabel would come up to feed with the other geese within a few yards of me, and if in the course of the winter I managed to create some impression upon her, it was perhaps more the bucket of corn which I usually carried than my personal charm that created it.

In February the geese, which had wintered in their thousands in the neighbourhood, started their northward migration, and by mid-March no pink-feet remained near the lighthouse save the twenty-nine pinioned ones —and Anabel. She seemed to find the sea pool, the salting grass, the shelter of the bank and the lighthouse, the fresh water pond, and, above all, a daily cropful of corn, exactly to her liking. From time to time she would fly round, but she did not seem particularly restless, and I had gradually come to think that she would probably stay right through the summer. Then, on the morning of May 16th, when I went out to feed the birds, there was no sign of Anabel. During the night she had slipped away and set off northwards to catch up with the great flocks which must already have left Scotland for the far north.

Greenland, Spitzbergen, and Iceland, the breeding grounds of all the pink-feet in the world, are dangerous places for a single goose. There are arctic foxes, and falcons, and men, for all of whom a goose is just a very good meal. As October began I became apprehensive. There were also the dangers of the early autumn to be overcome, when the geese are stubbling in Scotland, and later in Yorkshire; a hundred possible fates might have overtaken Anabel. But none of them had, and, at noon on October 9th, 1937, I heard her shout high up in a dappled autumn sky. She was a tiny

THE LIGHTHOUSE AT HIGH TIDE *Oil Painting 18″ × 15″*

PINKFEET PAIRED *Oil Painting 24" × 24"*

speck when I first saw her, almost straight above me, and with bowed wings she hurtled downwards. She came in confidently, without circling at all, and settled at the foot of the bank twenty yards from where I stood with my bucket of corn. I called to her and she walked straight up to me. Any doubt which I might have had that it was indeed Anabel was at once dispelled. There she stood, a plump little round person, with her queer angular forehead, her unusually pink bill pattern, and the few white feathers at its base. To me she was as recognisable as a stray sheep to a shepherd, or a stray hound to a huntsman.

So Anabel was back; she had been away for four months and twenty-four days. The very day she came, my friend Michael was broadcasting a talk about the geese and ducks on his marsh on the west coast. I sent him a telegram and at the end of his talk he read it out and told listeners about Anabel. This was less than seven hours after her arrival. A week later I chanced to be broadcasting, and was able to tell the story of her return more fully, so that Anabel became quite well known. She stayed again through the winter, with the birds at the lighthouse. Several other wild pinkfeet came in to join the throng, sometimes singly, sometimes in pairs and occasionally in small bunches. Anabel often flew round with them, but she knew that the lighthouse enclosure was her real home. When the others went off, as most of them did, with the departure of the main mass of the pinkfeet in February, Anabel stayed behind and came up to feed when she was called, with the pinioned birds. Although she led a sheltered life, safe from all enemies and with regular meals, hers was not a dull one. With her lived a hundred and fifty wild geese from all parts of the world, to say nothing of a crowd of ducks. Many of her neighbours were not at all easy to get on with; disagreements, quarrels and occasionally (though, of course, only amongst the more ill-bred members of the community) there were even fights, but there were compensations too, for few pinkfeet, after all, have had the opportunity of hob-nobbing with an Emperor goose.

I was ready for Anabel's departure in the spring, and just as she had gone the year before, again she slipped away during the night, and on the morning of May 10th her familiar dumpy figure was nowhere to be seen.

During the last week or two Anabel's companion on her short flights round about the lighthouse had been a big gander who had been caught in a flight net a year and a half before. Instead of being permanently pinioned in the usual way, after which the flight feathers of one wing can never grow again, he had only had the feathers clipped. In the autumn he moulted out the cut feather bases and grew fresh feathers so that he could fly again. In spite of that, however, he stayed all winter through, and on the morning of May 10th, the morning after Anabel's departure, he came to feed as usual. He has spent the whole summer at the lighthouse. It seems that the interruption of his migration for one season was enough, in his case, to make the migratory urge less strong than the urge to remain with the flock. With Anabel it was the other way round, although the migratory urge did not become strong enough to make her leave until mid-May, more than two months after the big flocks had gone northwards. Geese as individuals are very variable in character and it may be that, although the big gander decided to spend the summer at the lighthouse, others of his kind in like circumstances would have eloped with Anabel.

It is almost certain that geese do not usually breed until they are three years old, and Anabel is only two. If she survives this summer's dangers in the far north, and next summer's too, then in October 1939, perhaps, she will bring her first family with her to spend the winter in the lighthouse pen.

WIGEON AT THE EDGE OF THE SALTING AT MOON RISE *Oil Painting 30″ × 20″*

GREYLAGS AT CHAPEL ISLAND *Oil Painting 30″ × 20″*

CHAPTER THREE

BROGDEN

FIVE hundred greylags spend their winter days grazing mostly on Brogden's fresh green grass. The great marsh is separated from the estuary by two sea walls, an old one, now partly washed away, and a newer one in good repair a hundred yards inside it, which keeps the high tides out. But in spite of its reclamation from the sea there are pools and puddles on the marsh during the winter and the grass round them has a special attraction for the geese.

Eight years ago Brogden, though private, was not protected, and wildfowlers roamed all over it. Geese were rarely seen except in small bunches and they were 'here today and gone tomorrow'. But Michael took over the four hundred acres of land and gave the geese some measure of protection. Under the new régime the marsh was only shot occasionally, and in between whiles the geese were undisturbed. So the numbers which came there increased every year until one day last autumn we saw nearly eight hundred feeding between the cowhouse and the trough. These are the chief landmarks on the almost unbroken expanse of marsh. There are others—a big ditch down one side of the marsh, a railway embankment along the other, a wood on some rocks in one corner, and a wooded hill at the back. There is a broken-down wall and an old fence and lots of smaller ditches, a bridge over the big one, a chicken house, and now a small pond out in the middle specially dammed to attract ducks at evening flight when there has not been much rain and the surface of the marsh itself is not flooded.

I must have waited for geese there during more than a hundred dawns, so I have many memories of Brogden, and one of my pleasantest is of a bitter morning in December.

'You know the marsh; you'd better have a roving commission in the big ditch,' Michael had said when we left the car, and so I had been free to choose my exact position anywhere along the most likely quarter-mile of the big ditch, just below the bridge, where the geese might cross it on their way in to feed. We could hear them calling out on the sand as soon as we arrived.

As I splashed through the puddles towards my place, mallards got up in front of me, and snipe which had been roosting there, and a whistle of wigeon came across the marsh from near the cowhouse where the others were getting into position.

It was quite dark when I got to the big ditch. We usually arrived much too early, for most of the geese flighted fairly late, but occasionally an early lot, more thrilling than the others, would come unexpectedly out of the twilight, with hardly a heralding call.

Just such a party came in on this morning. I first knew of their coming by a low 'gung-gung' which sounded close in front; then suddenly they appeared flying quite low and straight towards me and one fell as they crossed the big ditch. They disappeared again into the darkness and I could trace them by their call as they swung round and headed out again towards the sand.

After that there was a long pause as the dawn broke behind the Westmorland hills, and then the real flight began. They were going mostly to the far end of the marsh where a good many shots were being fired. One lot only came to my end. I ran frantically down the ditch to try to be under them and missed them clean when I got there.

For a few minutes the air seemed to be full of geese, small parties, large parties, twos and threes, flying mostly rather high, for the morning was still and the noise of every shot carried far across the marsh.

It is a short flight from the sand on to the marsh, for the two are only separated by the two sea walls and the drainage cut which runs between them, but it is astonishing how high the geese will fly if they have once heard a shot.

In a few minutes most of the geese had returned to the sand to wait until the coast was clear before trying to come in again. During such a pause as this Michael makes it a strict rule that the marsh shall be left so that the geese can come in for the second time unmolested, and this, I believe, is the reason why the geese are not driven away.

Just as we were thinking about leaving on this December morning a small late lot of geese came in quite low and headed towards the big ditch. I dropped back into cover and shot a right and left as they came past, and then as soon as I had picked them up I set off with my three geese back towards the car. We all converged on the homeward walk, carrying altogether eight geese.

Before we had gone far the second flight began, and the geese were coming in high from the sand. As we reached the car we saw a big lot shimmering in the morning sun as they settled near the cowhouse, and we knew that in half an hour four hundred greylags would be feeding peacefully in the marsh we had just left.

Brogden is little more than a mile from the Ship Inn which is our headquarters in Westmorland; they lie just across the bay from one another, but the journey is seven miles by car round the head of the estuary.

Up the bay is where the wigeon sit during the day, and early in the season there are sometimes fine crowds of mallard and of teal. Their favourite stretch is less than a mile from the Ship, and the best shot we have ever made with the punt at wigeon was fired by the Baron as I pushed him down the channel in a nor'westerly gale, whilst Michael and Brian looked on with glasses from the sitting-room window and gave a running commentary on the proceedings by telephone to John a hundred and twenty miles away at Stafford.

The second best shot was made by Michael himself no further from the Ship, though just below it, which is another place where the wigeon sit, particularly if they have been disturbed further up. This is where the geese roost too, though we have only very rarely stalked the geese with the punt, and then only when there were small bunches on the sand, so that the main mass was not disturbed.

BROGDEN

Opposite to Brogden, on the same side of the estuary as the Ship, but further down, there is a fine salt marsh, covered only by spring tides. The wigeon flight on to the grass at night, and were it not for the sheep and the turf cutters and the holiday-makers on Sundays, I believe the geese would go there too. As it is, one may sometimes see a small lot feeding there, but it is a rare sight.

Below this the estuary is cut by a railway viaduct over which the trains rumble, often just at flight time, drowning for a minute all other sounds.

Sometimes the geese feed at night in Brogden under the moon, and occasionally when the weather is rough the tide drives them on to the marsh even on pitch dark nights. At such times one may walk into them in the morning on the way to one's place. I remember a moonlight night in November when there were a few pink-feet amongst the greylags. Early in the season there are often thirty or forty stray pink-feet which have got mixed with the greylags on their way to their own special estuary, which is a little further south. On this night such a party came over as we were walking out. They came just within shot and we got one. My place that night was in a little butt built of the loose stones from a tumbledown wall, and Michael and John were each ensconced in enormous rum-barrels which we had sunk the previous summer in the wetter parts of the marsh.

The darker it is the more mysterious and romantic do wild geese become, and that is why, to me, moonlight flighting is the most exciting of all forms of shooting except, perhaps, moonlight punting. I still have a clear picture in my mind of the geese that night, swinging up from the cowhouse, curling round the end of my wall, and coming back over me looking almost like bumble bees in the darkness, for the sky was overcast and one could see no details of their shape.

We did not stay long on the marsh so as not to disturb the geese too much, and when we started back we were carrying, as far as I remember, six geese. We have been moonlighting on Brogden once or twice since then, but I shall always remember that first night and the right and left of greylags which fell beside the old wall.

BRENTS COMING ON TO THE ZOSTERA *Oil Painting 24" × 24"*

WIGEON ON WET MUD *Oil Painting 18″ × 15″*

Although the geese nearly always roost on the sand between Brogden and the Ship in the early part of the season, later on they take sometimes to flying over the bay at dusk, and on southwards for about seven miles to Leighton Moss, which is a great flooded valley of reeds with patches of open water. Here, enclosed by wooded hills, in the most unlikely surroundings the geese roost, and in the dawn flight back to Brogden.

Waiting for the geese at Leighton is a strange thrill, unlike any other goose shooting that I know, for Leighton is a typical duck marsh, full of teal and shovelers (as well as almost every other kind of duck from mallard to smew).

The geese have their special pools on Leighton to which they come at dusk, but the most enjoyable evening I ever spent there was not beside one of these pools. It was in the centre of a line of butts called the hedge butts, and mine was the only one that was occupied. Indeed I was the only gun at that end of the marsh. Evening flight for ducks was usually rather disappointing at Leighton, but on this particular evening for a few minutes the sky was full of wings half seen and almost unheard above the noise of the wind in the reeds.

It was a rough night with driving sleet, and the ducks seemed to appear from nowhere, hang for an instant in the wind, and then swing away again into the darkness.

Suddenly I heard the geese. I had expected them to go to the other half of the marsh, whence I should have heard no sound of them against the wind, but now they were somewhere quite close and working upwind towards me. I waited, straining my eyes into the darkness, and then at last I made out the black smudge of them, fifty or sixty in a skein, heading to pass on my left. They were just too far and I was watching them with disappointment when a sudden call made me swing round. A single goose, flying on the flank of the main lot, was coming straight to me, and a moment later he had fallen stone dead amongst the reeds.

As we waded home against the wind with eleven ducks and a goose, and the sleet stinging our faces, Roger the keeper and I agreed that it had been a good flight. Bing, his dog, splashed along a yard or two in front, eager for a fireside which he had richly earned, for he had not lost a single duck that night. 'But you know, sir,' said Roger, turning to me, 'there's many people would say we were a couple of bloody fools to be out on a night like this, and enjoying it!'

When the geese first come to Brogden at the end of October they fly low over the sea wall and we stand at dawn behind it. As it gets light one may see the geese that remain on the sand and watch the little parties as they take wing and head in towards the marsh. At first they are silhouetted against the wet sand, but presently they disappear against the dark background of the hill beyond the estuary, and only reappear when they rise above the sky line; if they are flying low this is not until they are quite close, and there is little time to intercept them by running behind the bank. So usually we try to decide which way they will come during the very first part of their flight before they become invisible against the hill. Then we run helter-skelter along the back of the bank. Often two of us converge and meet and then there are shouts of 'too far', 'go back', 'behind you', and the like. How often have I wished that I had stayed exactly where I was! But with only three or four guns to cover three-quarters of a mile of bank, I think running will always be the order of the day behind Brogden's wall.

Outside the sea wall itself is a strip of grass to which the wigeon come both by night and by day, and next to that is 'the cut', which is the drainage water of the marsh. After it has passed through the sluice at one end of the marsh, 'the cut' runs the whole length of the front, bounded on the inside by the strip of salt grass and on the outside by the old sea wall, made mostly of stone and broken down in many places. There is an old butt built up in the stone which is just at the point where the geese most often cross to and from the marsh and also quite near the favourite patch of grass for the wigeon. Michael has had some good flights of wigeon there on rough mornings, and once he was especially well placed there for the geese. Coming from the sand

WIGEON BY MOONLIGHT *Oil Painting 18″ × 15″*

MALLARDS ARRIVING *Oil Painting 30″ × 20″*

the geese were swept into the marsh by half a gale of wind from the south-east and the two guns in the butts on the marsh were making a nasty hash of the flight. The startled geese returned to the sand low against the head wind over the butt on the old wall, and in a few minutes Michael had shot ten. One of these was a barnacle goose, the only one that we have ever seen amongst the greylags on Brogden. Whitefronts come occasionally to the marsh and two have been shot there, and last winter a single brent goose appeared with the grey geese, and stayed for a week or two on the marsh. It is interesting to speculate upon how these strangers first became attached to the flocks which they accompany. Perhaps it is at some point where the migration routes of the two species cross, or perhaps it originates even further north, in a common breeding area.

Last March a party of four geese arrived at the lighthouse and stayed for a week before flying off northward. They were three pink-footed geese and one barnacle. In the extraordinary way which geese have of knowing not only where danger is, but where it is not, they became quite tame and one could walk up to within fifteen yards before they would bother to fly, and then they would only flip up and settle again on the other side of the pen. At that time, including Anabel and others, there were about a dozen full-winged geese at the lighthouse, and occasionally a whole bunch of them would get up and fly round together.

Now the interesting thing about this barnacle goose is that he would have nothing to say to the ten pinioned barnacles which live at the lighthouse. Evidently he had consorted all winter with his three pink-footed companions, and since they joined the pink-foot flock he too browsed amongst the pink-feet, and did not appear even to notice the little party of barnacles which grazed on the other side of the creek. Since for a week he showed no signs of recognition of his own species one was left wondering whether he ever would return to the barnacle hosts should he meet with them in the far north.

When there is a frost the geese leave Brogden and the marsh is deserted. On such mornings one may make some compensation for their absence, as soon as it gets light, by walking up the running ditches for snipe. Otherwise one can seldom shoot snipe on Brogden for fear of disturbing the geese.

It was weather like this when Brian, who had never shot a goose, first came to Brogden in his Christmas holidays from school. But just before he was due to leave, the frost broke and the geese came back. On the last morning we went to the marsh as usual, long before dawn. We took Brian to a shallow butt which was half-full of water, and left him with last-minute instructions. 'Whatever you do, don't shoot at them till you think they'll knock your hat off': he had no hat, but he knew the meaning of the phrase. 'If you shoot too soon it'll spoil it for the others, so wait till you are absolutely sure of them.' 'All right!' 'Well, good luck!' 'Thanks, same to you!' 'Thanks!' And we wandered off to our places, the Baron to the trough, and I to the other little butt which had been called after me ever since I had, one morning, shot twelve geese from it the year before.

Unexpectedly the geese came early and in great packs. The first pack flew over Brian high, circled and flew over him low, then circled again and flew over him lower still, but no shot was fired. They swung round past the trough and the baron bagged one, and then they climbed and went out to the estuary again. The next lot did the same and again Brian did not fire. Such restraint was unheard of, and the Baron took a nice right and left at fully fifty yards as they curled away from the trough by which he hid. The next lot came to me and I shot one, and almost simultaneously I heard two shots from away on Brian's side of the marsh. As I looked, half a dozen geese, already far out of shot, were climbing yet higher into the sky.

Then came the pause which was the signal for our departure. All the geese had flighted once for the marsh and, having returned to the sand, were waiting until hunger should drive them to make another attempt. Brian came across the marsh to meet us as we set off for the car. Over his shoulder hung something which flapped as he walked. Was it a goose? It was better still—two geese. Apparently a low pair had come straight to him

PINKFEET AT HIGH-NOON *Oil Painting 20" × 30"*

and he had bagged them both handsomely. The half-dozen high ones which I had seen had merely chanced to be overhead at the time.

So Brian's first goose had been shot with his right barrel and his second goose an instant later with his left. They had fallen stone dead within five yards of each other—and we went home to a celebration breakfast.

at the edge of the tide, and they were barnacle geese, eighteen of them that we had somehow overlooked.

We pushed out and set off towards them. The sun was behind us, but below it the sand cliff was a dark background, and for once we were almost unnoticed as we pushed across the bay at top speed with the shortest setting-pole. At first success was a far-away thing, and then with glorious rapidity it became a possibility, a probability, almost a certainty, and—woomf—an accomplished fact.

As the smoke cleared away I sat up and pushed the boat into the shore without delay. It had been a good shot: but one goose was making off across the sand and I jumped out and gave chase. Only the tip of his wing was broken, the tip of his right wing. As I ran I felt sure, from the trailing primaries, that this would be a splendid bird to keep alive. Throughout the chase 'the pace was killing', and when I eventually caught up with him nearly half a mile from the punt, I sat down exhausted and panting on the sand with Bill exhausted and panting in my lap. The capture of Bill might well be the end of this story but actually it is the beginning, at any rate of that part of it which is strange and extraordinary.

Bill had the very tip joint of his right wing badly broken, and it was only a small operation to remove it altogether. On it grew the first four of the ten flight feathers or primaries. To stop a goose from flying, all its primaries must be cut, so with a pair of scissors I clipped the remaining six.

Now Michael, who lives in Cheshire, wanted to add a barnacle to his collection of geese, so at once I sent Bill off by train, with a warning to Michael that a year later, when the cut feathers were moulted out, he would be able to fly. In the meantime it would be wise to pinion him properly so that the remaining six primaries would not grow again.

Somehow the summer came round and Bill had not been pinioned. In July he moulted, and new wing feathers grew—all but the four at the very tip of his right wing. Even without these four he could fly fairly well, and during August he often made short flights round the enclosure. Then one September day he was gone. For a week Michael expected him to turn up again. Bill had probably, he thought, been blown away by the westerly equi-

WIGEON AND TEAL AT LEIGHTON

Oil Painting 55" × 33"

BARNACLES IN SHALLOW WATER *Oil Painting 24" × 24"*

noctial gales. A farmer would ring up to say he had caught a strange-looking duck on his farm, which was now in a bag in his barn, and would Michael kindly come and fetch it. But no such message came, and Bill was lost.

It was about five weeks later that, running my eye over the little flock of pinioned barnacle geese which live amongst the many other kinds on the saltmarsh at the lighthouse, I noticed that there were ten instead of nine. When we walked out to look at them near to, we expected the newcomer to be a wild one, and to fly off; but we walked close to them and none flew. Indeed, we could not pick out the new arrival because they all seemed to be pinioned. When eventually they flapped away one was just able to lift, and fly across the creek, though he was rather lop-sided.

We herded them all into a corner and caught the stranger with a hand-net. From his right wing the first four primaries were missing. The primary coverts on the under side of the wing, the smaller feathers which overlap the bases of the flight feathers themselves, had not been moulted and bore the marks where they had been cut with scissors, showing that the other six primaries must have been clipped sometime during the year before the July moult.

The lighthouse is about 150 miles from Michael's home in Cheshire, in a south-easterly direction. During that September and October there were westerly gales, and it was the season of the year when the instinct of a barnacle goose would lead it southward with the approach of winter.

Was this newcomer our old friend Bill? I am inclined to believe that he was, because barnacle geese are rare enough in captivity for the coincidence to be even greater, should one assume that during those five weeks there were two barnacle geese at large without the first four primaries of their right wings.

Ours is pinioned now, and we call him Bill anyway.

CHAPTER FIVE

GREAT OCCASIONS

I believe that all moments of great happiness should be recorded in a diary, no matter how private it may become, not because any man should wallow in the past and sigh for the good old days, but because memory is such an unreliable part of our mental equipment, and so much of joy and happiness in life slips into the mists and is lost for ever. So the diary should be put away and the happiness banked against a day of trouble or sadness.

The diary would have many records of achievements, and I believe often they would be quite small and unimportant achievements, whilst bigger ones would go unrecorded. It might be a big trout that had at last been caught, a worthy opponent beaten at chess, a rare plant persuaded at last to flower.

I'm afraid I do not keep a diary like this, but if I did I think one of the greatest occasions would be an August afternoon at Lowestoft when 'Thunder', my International 14 ft. dinghy, crossed the finishing line first by sixteen seconds in the championship race for the Prince of Wales' Cup. The race itself, which lasted about three hours, had been especially thrilling. My best friend had been second, and for me it was the climax of four years of trying. I am not likely to forget the thrill of those first few minutes after the gun when my crew and I kept reminding and assuring each other that we really had won. We had gone into first place only in the last two hundred yards of the fifteen mile course, so that the possibility of winning did not have time to sink in until long after we had actually finished. But although I shall not forget this thrill, I wish that I had written down every little tiny detail of what it felt like, that very evening, to re-read long years hence.

After 'Thunder', in that 1937 championship race, came 'Lightning', sailed by John Winter. In 'Lightning' he had won the Prince of Wales' Cup

THE ISLAND POOL AT LEIGHTON

Oil Painting 18″ × 15″

in 1934, and had been runner-up each year since. Third was 'Alarm', sailed by Stewart Morris, who had been champion no less than four times.

Were I to look through my imaginary diary I should find these two figuring in very different circumstances on an October day two years earlier.

The day dawned, for us, across Leighton Moss in Westmorland, one of the most beautiful duck marshes in England. It was a bright still morning and my place was in a butt by a pool on what was called the 'Red road', a pathway cut in the rushes along which one must wade in six inches of water to the low hide formed by growing willows. With me came Stewart as a spectator. It was his first experience of a morning flight of ducks.

As we splashed out along the 'Red road' the marsh seemed alive with mallards. They got up with a clatter and quack in ones and twos and bevies all round us, but it was too early to see them: only the faintest grey showed above the dark line of hills to the east. After we had arrived at the butt there was, at first, a deep silence by contrast to our noisy wading. Then in the far distance we could hear the quacking of ducks as they rose in alarm, disturbed by the others of the party on the way to their places, amongst them John. As the paleness spread across the sky we heard a whistle far above, and almost in a moment the air was full of wings. The wigeon were returning from the puddles amongst the grass fields and the tide pools on the saltings. They swept in in parties of twenty and thirty. Over me they came too high, and I watched them pass on towards the guns on the causeway, half way up the marsh.

It was quite light before a shoveler came in to the pool by the 'Red road' and gave me my first shot. After that the teal began to appear, from nowhere it seemed. They came in twos and threes low over the reeds and they disappeared again against the dark hills. There was only a moment to shoot and that was when they were at their closest, and the charge of shot spread no larger than a cricket-ball.

Stewart kept watch towards the dawn whilst I watched carefully the darker half of the sky. The teal still came when it was broad daylight, and occasional shovelers came too, but there were no mallards. Since their departure in the darkness only a pair had appeared, and they had circled high over the marsh and then gone off again.

At breakfast time we made our way to the little hut which stands by the road where we leave the cars. In spite of our late start, our score was the best: exactly twenty birds, which were mostly teal. It was at that time the most ducks that I had ever shot at a single flight. But in other parts of the marsh the bag had been a good one too, and every one of the other guns had had a splendid flight.

The day was yet young and we had another plan in hand. John had never shot a stag, and we had some stalking on a small forest up in the Lakes. So after a hurried breakfast we drove furiously to the rendezvous with the old stalker who was a Scotsman and very deaf. Stewart came too, again as a spectator, and with stalker and gillie the five of us began to climb the steep slope which led to a summit at the south end of the ground, the best spying place with a north-west wind.

When we were half-way up, Stewart said that he had developed a higher opinion of Everest climbers than he had previously held.

But at the top we were rewarded with a magnificent view out over Ullswater to the slopes of Martindale, the greatest of the Lake deer forests. We spied across our own ground, which was a little plateau of steeply rolling hillocks with deep gullies between. There was one small party of deer in sight about three-quarters of a mile away. It contained several good young stags and one switch-horn, a degenerate head of which the forest should be rid. He was a fairly heavy stag, so it seemed, and very dark coloured, and it was undoubtedly our duty to select him rather than any other stag for our stalk.

I have long held the view that the professional stalker is the man who gets the best fun out of deer-stalking, and on this occasion I was determined that I should have that fun and try myself to take John in to shoot his first stag.

I had told my plan to the old stalker, who received it with a grunt, which might have meant that he had not heard what I said or that he simply disapproved. Anyway, by now the sole argument against the plan, the possibility that I might not select a suitable beast to shoot, had been removed because the stag was already selected.

But it was no use, for no sooner had we finished spying than, beckoning us to follow, the old man led us down the slope and along the side of a ridge. Further along we were able to cross the ridge where a buttress from the slope beyond came between us and the deer. For twenty minutes we hurried after him not knowing at all what point he wanted to reach, nor how he intended to reach it, and it was useless to ask him, for no whispered question could he hear.

Along a steep slope we crawled in single file until at last he stopped. John crawled up on one side of him and I on the other, and there were the deer lying down below us and fully two hundred yards away. I shook my head to indicate that it was too far. We had the day before us and we could try another approach.

This way we could get no closer. So in single file we crawled away again, and from a neighbouring knoll surveyed the deer, looking for a different way to stalk. The only one seemed to be over the very hillock on the slope of which they lay. We should appear within thirty yards, but well above them.

The stalker set off again, but this time we were in a strong position, because somehow I had gained possession of the rifle.

So when he strode off he went alone. After going fifty yards, he turned and saw us still sitting on the knoll and he knew that we had won. As good as gold he came back and agreed to sit and watch us whilst we went forth to stalk by ourselves.

One stalk is very much like another, unless you happen to have been doing it yourself. Ours was a very exciting one, which lasted more than two hours. It included meeting one of the smaller stags of our party face to face at fifty yards, when neither of us expected the other; it included a hectic interlude following up the now suspicious deer, and a lot of crawling to avoid being seen by some new deer which had appeared on a neighbouring ridge. Towards the end it included half an hour of 'inch-at-a-time' crawling on our tummies, and just to finish up with we had a 'hands-and-knees'

CHAPTER SIX

TWELVE HOURS AFLOAT

IT was blowing hard when the four of us pushed off from the quay, two in each punt. We rowed across to the weather shore and then drifted down under the lee of the high marsh. It was a really strong wind and we doubted whether we should be able to carry out our plan, because the open water would be too rough. Our side of the river was well sheltered for it was already half ebb and we were swept down by the tide, rowing a little to keep ourselves near the bank. After a mile we were below the marsh, but on our side there was still a steep cliff of sand, and on the top of it sat a spring of teal. They were a few yards back from the top and we drifted down, crouching in the punts with our four hand guns ready. The punt gun could not have been brought to bear, and anyway there were only very few teal. Our plan was a success, and although the day was no more than just begun we had seven teal aboard as we rowed on down the channel.

Round the corner a magnificent black line could be seen stretching across the sand—over a thousand ducks which were mostly pintails and wigeon with a sprinkling of mallards and a few outlying bunches of teal and shovelers. But alas! we were almost too late. Half an hour earlier these birds would have been within reach of the channel, but now the tide had ebbed away from them and they were left far back on the sand.

At the far end, however, some were still at the water's edge and there might be a chance of a shot provided that we could pass the others on the shore without disturbing them. It was not a chance for a double stalk with both punts, so John and I set off with one. We lay down and then pushed out round the corner.

The chance seemed a poor one, but we had a splendid, though tantalising, view of the massed ducks, huddled together for shelter from the wind, as we passed them broadside on. They were only just out of range of the water. Miraculously they let us slip past, and the pintails and shovelers at the edge of the water ahead, though a little wild, were well bunched. John timed the shot beautifully and the bag after twenty minutes' hard rowing and running on shore was twenty-five birds.

An hour later we tried an unsuccessful stalk at some mallards sitting on a sandy islet, but the water was too shallow and we ran aground. Out in the channel behind us was a tight little bunch of about sixty scaups, diving no doubt for mussels. We watched them for a few minutes, for to us they were unfamiliar, except as odd birds or in twos and threes on the Wash.

Then in the far distance we heard the call of approaching geese and a minute later three hundred barnacles came across the estuary flying high. Just beyond us they swung round and circled down on to the high sand a few hundred yards away.

Meantime the tide was still falling and we found that our punt was hard and fast: there was nothing to do but jump out and pull her off before it was too late. The scaups were very tame. As we stood up they only swam away down channel, whereas of course the game ducks, our quarry, were off upon the instant. The geese were just too far away to be upset by us, and we hoped that later on they might walk down to the water's edge where we should have a chance to go after them. We spied to see if anything were below us and a black patch on the next point turned out to be three hundred teal sitting as we had seldom seen teal sit before. We lay down at once and then set off at full speed with very high hopes. It was a rare chance. The stalk was easy as the shore was beautifully shelving and the bottom was nice hard sand. The wind had abated considerably and the light was perfect. We were still three hundred yards away when they jumped for no apparent reason at all, and pitched in the water beyond the point. In a few minutes the wind and the tide had drifted them round the corner and out of sight.

We waited for the other punt to come up. They had been lying down hoping for the barnacles to come to the water's edge and they had so far waited in vain. We ate some sandwiches and agreed that the wind had decreased sufficiently in strength to allow us to proceed with our plan. It was that one punt should return up our own river with the flood tide, whilst the other went further down, turned left along the open channel and at flood tide came up a neighbouring river where it would be met by the car some hours after dark.

So half an hour later we said farewell to our sister craft and John and I set off for our great sea passage. We hoped that the teal would have gone ashore again by now round the corner, for teal like most ducks are usually worth nothing to the punt-gunner when they are afloat; and in case they had done so we lay down and stalked gingerly round the point. It was a thrilling moment as we gradually opened out the shore beyond, and more thrilling still when we saw that our hopes had been fulfilled. There they all sat tightly bunched as a shelter from the wind amongst a dozen or two mallards which had probably been there all the time. About thirty of the teal were in a round bunch a little nearer to us than the main lot, but we resolutely passed these by within easy shot. We were ambitious and the birds beyond sat proverbially 'like jam in a jar'. But the mallards were our downfall. Mallards are usually wilder than teal and quicker to observe the approach of a punt, but they are also more likely to remain standing, watching the punt for those last fatal moments when it is drawing within shot. Teal on the other hand jump upon impulse and with no preliminary head-raising. The combination was the salvation of the ducks, for the instant that the mallards raised their heads the teal took wing and the mallards went with them. In a fraction of a second a grand chance was transformed into a 'might-have-been'. We sat up in the punt agreeing that *if* we had been quick enough we might even as it was have bagged twenty, but it was a big 'if'.

The teal split up and some of them went out on to the open water whilst others went back up the river behind us. So we hoisted sail to go about three miles to the mouth of the little river that would lead us back to land.

THE EARLIEST ARRIVALS AT EVENING FLIGHT *Oil Painting 18″ × 15″*

Its mouth was difficult to find, because at low tide it was no more than a trickle and it ran out over the sand as a delta with only an inch or two of water anywhere. The upper waters, we knew, were deeper and navigable, and this was where the mallards sat and occasionally, at dawn and dusk, the barnacles. It was doubtful if the tide would have flowed enough to float us over the delta and into the navigable water before it became too dark to see, and when at last we came to the mouth and recognised it as our turning, the doubt became a certainty. Already the November evening was upon us and the tide must rise fully two feet before we could hope to float over the rapids of the delta and into the sluggish reach where there was always at least ten inches of water.

We anchored the punt at the mouth and walked up the river in the gathering darkness, taking with us the glasses to see if there were any ducks about, but there were practically none. The little channel wore a deserted and desolate air. Half a mile from the punt nine or ten mallards straggled on one bank, but they would not have been worth a stalk, even had we been able to float over the delta and push up to them. We strolled back to the punt disappointed that there was so little about and yet glad that we had not been tantalised by seeing a fine bunch of birds just beyond reach.

It was a cold grey evening and the wind had freshened again. We were about four miles from our destination and we knew that it would take us nearly four hours to get there, so sluggish were the neap tides at that time.

It is a tedious business waiting for the tide at night. One presses forward until the punt grounds, then waits a few minutes for water to float in and presses forward again, pushing with a pole, which always seems to me to be the easiest way in sandy estuaries. But there is another difficulty which arises in the dark. When the punt grounds it does not necessarily do so on the lowest sand. Sometimes it grounds upon a sort of island. It may take some time to be floated over this island, and meanwhile the tide has found the deepest part of the channel and swept on ahead so that, in front, there is an expanse of water and the true channel is lost. One may find oneself waiting to be floated up some minor lead or runnel when to remain in the channel one should have turned sharply to the left. So the way at night must be especially carefully watched. If one goes far out of one's way it is hard to know on which side to look for the channel one has lost, and to regain it involves going forth into the open and perhaps rough water of the tide which is following so closely on one's heels.

So it was on this November night that one of us must constantly wander away from the punt to check the depth of the channel ahead, to make sure it was the right one, and if it were not, to walk out first on one side, and then on the other to find it. The other waited in the punt to answer the call of the returning pathfinder, for the night was very dark. Even this could not be heard at any great distance as the wind was strong and the waves broke behind us along the edge of the tide.

For two hours we worked slowly up the stream, waiting in the cold and walking out to make sure of our way, and then the channel became more obvious and also more familiar. I walked a little way ahead and some mallards rose up quacking in the darkness. I wondered what they were doing out there at that time, for they should have been with their brethren feeding in the marshes. By now a feeble moon was showing patchily behind the hurrying clouds, and the wind was stronger than ever. I returned to help the punt over a shallow and into a long lagoon, and then we came in amongst some roosting gulls. They rose silently quite close to us on all sides.

A few moments later we noticed what we took to be a sand cliff showing black ahead of us. I knew that there had been no sand cliff there some days before, but I knew also that these river channels changed from day to day. On the off chance that they were birds (and geese were the only birds they could have been), we lay hurriedly down in the punt and cocked the big gun. As we pushed in towards that rectangular black bar, which seemed to be terribly close and so high that it could not possibly be other than a vertical sand cliff, there suddenly came, clear and loud, a single bark that brought our hearts into our mouths—the bark of a barnacle. It is almost impossible to describe the excitement which took hold of us both at that moment, when we had almost decided that we were stalking a sand cliff. They *were* geese and they were hardly thirty paces

PINTAILS AND TEAL *Oil Painting 30" × 20"*

BARNACLES DISTURBED *Oil Painting 18″ × 15″*

from us. All at once the black bar was doubled in height as fifty barnacles raised their heads simultaneously; and half a second later came that most disastrous of all sounds to the punt-gunner, the click of a gun that has misfired.

John grabbed at the hammer and recocked. The barnacles were up and swinging back on the wind. For an instant the barrel of the big gun seemed to wave wildly in the air and in the next there was a blinding burst of orange flame and a thunderous roar as, this time, the cap responded to the tug on the trigger lanyard.

John was out of the punt and rushing forward in the shallow water almost before our eyes had recovered from the flash. Dimly I could see him running after a wounded bird, whilst some dark objects on the water seemed to indicate that, in spite of the misfire, we had done quite well. A minute or two later I saw him coming back and walked out to meet him. 'I've got seven here and there are two more to get,' he said. So whilst he went back to the punt I waded on to pick up the other two. Nine barnacle geese for a flying shot, and a high one at that, was not so bad, and even if the gun had gone off the first time I believe that we should have got no more. They would have been much too close.

We reloaded the big gun, for we had still a mile and a half of likely water to traverse before reaching the marsh and it was possible, though unlikely, that some birds might settle again on the channel ahead. We lay down and stalked the rest of the way on the off-chance, but we saw nothing. Then, just as we came to the marsh, we saw the headlights of the car shining from the farmyard and, soon after, were hailed out of the gloom by Michael and the Baron.

It was after nine on a dark and windy night when we anchored our punt below the marsh-edge, just twelve hours after we had embarked.

CHAPTER SEVEN

THE RAILWAY BRIDGE

IN punt gunning the worst dangers are the unexpected ones.

If you set out to make a rough passage across an estuary with a strong wind against an ebb tide you are probably expecting trouble, and if you are sensible you will turn back before the boat starts to fill up faster than you can bale. You are much more likely to be drowned when you least expect it, when you are stupid enough to be anchored when the flood tide hits you, or when you try to shoot a rapid in the dark.

On a certain Boxing Day we launched two double punts on a northern estuary. We launched them in the darkness in a river pool just above the Railway Bridge, and since the tide was well out and there seemed to be very little water running over the rocky sill underneath the bridge we decided to pull them over the slippery concrete at one side.

When this had been successfully accomplished we sped away down stream to reach the bend where the greylags came to wash at dawn.

Dawn sometimes comes slowly and sometimes fast, or so it seems, and on this morning it came more slowly than ever. As we left the Railway Bridge there was already a grey light behind the hills and we rowed as hard as we could lest the geese should have flighted to the marsh before we could get there.

Yet as we neared the place it was still too dark to see. There were a few rocky islets in the channel and one or two mallards got up as we passed them. The geese should have been half a mile further on, but suddenly we heard a 'honk' in front and unexpectedly half a dozen loomed up no more than sixty yards away. There were not enough to make a shot and almost as soon as we saw them they swam out and then took wing. Further on the geese were far out on the high sand away from the channel.

We waited for the light, so that the ducks, which were arriving from their night's feeding inland, should have time to get settled into big parties, and we should be able to see where they were and how we should stalk them.

In one punt were Michael and Johnny, and in the other Brian, on his holiday from school, and me.

Michael and Johnny tried the first stalk with the small gun at some mallards and it was not a success. It never looked a great chance as they drifted round a sharp bend in the channel, but they ought to have got more than three. It was just one of those strange and inexplicable failures.

Half an hour later Brian and I were rapidly approaching a very fine crowd of wigeon sitting 'like jam in a jar' at the channel's edge nearly a mile further down. Just as we drew into range the pushing became terribly hard work and I realised that the flood tide had arrived. At the same time some of the wigeon were floated off and began to swim about. For the last few yards I pushed with redoubled effort and we took a flying shot as they lifted. Immediately we pushed forward to pick up as quickly as possible, for what had been a shallow sandy channel about thirty yards wide was becoming a sweeping and ever increasing expanse of water in which it was more and more difficult to manage the punt.

I set Brian ashore on one side to collect the dead birds and crossed over to go after two or three wounded ones which were making off. But single-handed in that swift tide I found the punt unmanageable, and since the other punt had at last arrived on the scene, I shouted that they should take Brian across after the cripples whilst I returned to pick up the rest.

I watched them rowing out and when they had almost reached the shore I watched Brian step out of the punt on the wrong side. He had made no allowance for the speed of the tide and the punt was swept onto him, knocking him down. He picked himself up dripping and set off on foot, wading after the rapidly disappearing wigeon. It was quite clear that he could never catch them, as in two feet of water he could never wade fast enough to catch up the edge of the tide, which constantly retreated in front of him, and eventually when he actually began to lose ground the other punt had to row out and pick him up again. Rain had in the meantime set in, though during these hectic minutes it had been quite unnoticed. Brian, after his ducking, did not care much anyway.

There was no more to be done that day in the rain and we set off for home.

The tide was well in under the Railway Bridge half an hour later as we rowed back under it to the launching place and landed thirty-one wigeon and six mallards from our last shot and three more mallards from the first one. Then we motored home to change and have lunch. After lunch the weather cleared a little and we decided to take a dog and to hunt the marshes opposite the place of our big shot, whither the tide should have taken the two wounded birds which had escaped. We decided too that it would be a good plan, when the tide was still in the pool, to take the two punts through the Railway Bridge and tie them up just below. This would obviate scraping them on the concrete sill in the darkness of the following morning and the accompanying hard work.

It was after four o'clock when we turned off the main road and followed a mile and a half of lane to the little salting where I planned to look for the wounded ducks from our morning's punt shot. Michael and Brian dropped me and Buoy, my Labrador, and went off the few miles round to the head of the estuary to take the two punts through the bridge and return for me when they had done it. It was beginning to get dark as I wandered along the marsh hunting in the creeks. A few mallards were flighting inland and a party of wigeon swept along the edge of the sand. I returned through the rushy grass behind the marsh. Buoy picked up a rabbit and brought it to me, but there was no sign of the ducks. I came back to the end of the road watching for the headlights of the returning car. A little mist was coming up, but overhead it was clear sky and there were bright stars. I cast along the shore in the other direction with the dog and found nothing ; and then I returned again to the road and sat down on a boulder to wait. I wondered what could be keeping them so long and whether they had missed the entrance to the little lane in the mist. They had already been away for an hour and a half.

Out on the bay I could hear the geese settling down for the night. They had come down from higher up as the tide uncovered their favourite bank about three-quarters of a mile away.

I started to wander up the lane towards the main road and as I went I walked faster and faster.

The origins of panic are strange. For the first few hundred yards I was

GREYLAGS LEAVING THE MUD AT DAWN — *Oil Painting 30" × 20"*

wondering why they were taking so long, and before I had got half-way to the main road I was running as hard as I could in a blind panic. Something, I *knew*, had gone wrong, dangerously wrong. A motor accident was my guess. I was absolutely certain that something had happened to Michael and Brian, much worse than mere running out of petrol. Actually, I remembered, there wasn't much petrol in the car, and there were several stretches of deserted road where a 'run-out' would have made them at least as late as they were so far. But I was sure it was something worse than that and so I ran up the lane.

When I got to the top I didn't know what to do. There were two ways that the car might come and I could not risk missing it. So I paced up and down looking hopefully for the glare of approaching headlights, but none came.

Some men loomed up out of the mist and told me that there was a keeper's house with a telephone two hundred yards away, and one of them volunteered to keep watch at the turning, should the car arrive whilst I was gone.

The keeper was very kind and with his telephone I put through a call to the Post Office of the village near the Railway Bridge. I knew the name of the man whose house overlooked the pool above the bridge, who had helped us to unload our ducks so very many hours, it seemed, before. I asked the Post Office to get him if possible to the telephone and to ring me back, and then I waited and as I waited all my fears returned.

* * * * *

Three hours earlier, just at dusk, Michael and Brian arrived at the Railway Bridge. The tide had ebbed out rather further than they had expected and there was a dull roar of the water running over the sill under the middle span of the bridge.

It was too dark to see from the shore what the rapid was like, so they got into the punt to row out to look at it. Michael did not much like the look of it and said that he didn't think on the whole that it was worth risking. Brian said, 'Well, you'll never know if it's possible unless you try', and the next moment the punt was swept under the bridge. If they had been just half an hour earlier all would probably have been well, but some of the boulders were already breaking surface and the punt struck and stuck fast half across the stream. The water piled up behind her and she began to fill fast. They both jumped out and, standing in the torrent, lifted the punt clear. As she floated off, waterlogged, Michael managed to scramble aboard, but as he did so the anchor slipped off the stern deck and held fast amongst the rocks. The punt drifted a few yards and then it was brought up short with a jerk in the white water below the rapid.

A waterlogged boat is a difficult thing to balance. With great care Michael crept into the stern, where the anchor rope was attached, but immediately the water ran aft and the stern was so low that the current piled up and over the stern deck and poured in so fast that he had to jump back into the bows.

The position was now rather serious, because Brian was standing twenty yards away with the swift water running well above his knees. The boulders were treacherously slippery, and he was in danger of being dashed against a rock and then swept down in the darkness into the deep pool below. Michael was balancing the punt in this pool with fifteen feet of water beneath him, expecting to founder at any minute.

He decided to try and swim ashore so that he could fetch a pole from the other punt and wade out to Brian's assistance. To this end he took off most of his clothes and cast them down. His coat was just being washed away when he remembered that in it was his wallet with a large sum of money, and just retrieved it in time. He stopped to think if there was anything at all he could do other than swim in that ice-cold river water, and he decided that it was just possible that the boat could be baled out before she actually turned over and was pulled down by the weight of the big gun.

First of all he shouted to Brian above the roar of the water, to stand perfectly still and not to try to wade ashore until the boat was properly afloat again, or until a setting pole could be passed to him so that he could feel his way. Then he set to work to bale the punt dry. In twenty minutes it was done, and Brian was still standing in the rapids. Michael could just see him dimly through the mist and darkness. He shouted to him again to be sure not to try to move, but he couldn't tell whether he had heard.

GREYLAGS AND THE STEEL WORKS

Oil Painting 30" × 20"

WIGEON AT HOLM MARSH *Oil Painting 30″ × 20″*

The next move was to try to get the anchor up. Michael moved aft and started to pull on the anchor rope. The punt was swinging a little in the current. He managed to pull her up a few feet on the anchor, but suddenly she swung into the fastest water and it piled up against the coamings. The next moment it was pouring over the stern again, and Michael was only just in time as he moved forward into the bows to save her from going down altogether. Again she was waterlogged, and one false move would have turned her upside down.

It looked after all as though the only thing to do would be to bale her dry again and then swim ashore. He was already wet enough, but on the other hand six o'clock on a December night was a poor time to go bathing under a lonely Railway Bridge.

He baled her out again, then decided to have one last try to get the anchor up. He got hold of the rope and gave a tug and again the water poured aboard, but just as he was letting go, suddenly the anchor slipped clear of the rocks and the punt was drifting into the eddy at the side of the pool.

Michael paddled her safely ashore. He took a couple of setting poles, which have pronged ends, and waded out carefully underneath the bridge. Brian had been very wise; he stood exactly where he had stepped out from the punt three-quarters of an hour earlier. Michael reached out and passed him one of the poles, and together, finding a firm bedding for the prongs of their poles at each stride, they worked their way towards the shore.

They lay down and rested because they were both exhausted, more by the strain than by the exertion, and a few minutes later they made their way to the car. Then Michael dressed himself in two motor rugs, one worn as a kilt and the other as a plaid. They were two different tartans and no doubt it would have made a Scotsman wince to see them together, but they kept Michael warm, which was the main thing.

They went to the house of our friend who had helped us unload the birds in the morning. He gave them some hot tea and warmed them through, and just as they were setting off he was called away to the telephone by the postmistress. They wondered for a moment whether this could be anything to do with them, and they decided that it couldn't. So they set off round the head of the estuary towards the little marsh where they had left me more than three hours before.

* * * * *

Sitting in the keeper's cottage I waited for the telephone to ring, and at last the call came through. My friends, I was told, had had some difficulty with the punts, but they were now quite all right and just starting off to fetch me. He would tell them to come to the keeper's cottage at the top of the little lane, instead of going right down to the marsh.

With relief I waited, going constantly to the door whenever I heard an approaching car. The mist had cleared a little and at last I saw them come up to the corner. They slowed down, turned into the lane, and sped away towards the marsh and I started after them on foot.

Ten minutes later I saw the headlights coming back towards me. They had evidently decided that I could not still be there. As the headlights came into a straight piece of the lane in front of me the car stopped, a hundred yards away, and when I reached them I learned that it had run out of petrol. So back we walked along that lane together, indulging our relief in an orgy of questions and explanations.

They were just as delighted to find that I was not lying in a creek on the marsh with a broken leg, as I was to see them safe and sound.

There was a 'bus passing along the main road and we thought of boarding it in search of petrol, until we suddenly remembered Michael's rather unconventional dress.

So we fell back on the keeper's telephone again, and waited for supplies of petrol to arrive whilst we very thankfully joined the keeper and his wife at the remains of their Christmas turkey.

FLOODTIDE ON A WINDY NIGHT *Oil Painting 30″ × 20″*

MALLARD DRAKE *Oil Painting 18″ × 15″*

CHAPTER EIGHT

BROADCASTING

WIRELESS will always be for me one of those inexplicable wonders, like the instincts of colonial insects, or the workings of a chess champion's mind, or higher mathematics, or the migration of birds. But even for those who do not understand its principles, it has invented new thrills. I can sit, for example, in my lighthouse and hear Toscanini conduct Verdi's Requiem. I could do that if I went to Queen's Hall, but without the B.B.C. I could not hear Howard Marshall say 'He's out!' at the end of Bradman's innings in a Test Match, not even if I went to Lords. Mr. Marshall's consummate skill makes those two words convey the biggest thrill in cricket, that someone has beaten the world's best batsman.

At the start of the Derby, too, or the Grand National, the wireless has one special moment, more exciting to the layman than the result itself, and that is when the commentator shouts 'They're off!'

By comparison with all these great events our little 'outside broadcast' was a very modest affair. We made a running commentary on the feeding of the ducks in St. James' Park. We put a microphone by the water's edge and tried to catch the calls of the ducks as they dibbled about in the shallow water on a summer Sunday afternoon.

An American to whom I mentioned our broadcast said, 'Oh, does that sort of thing "go across big" over here?' I had to admit that if it went across at all it certainly did not go big, but that we hoped that, if it went across even quite small, some people would like it.

The ducks behaved very well and about two hundred of them gathered together in the shallows and made cheerful noises quite near the microphone, whilst I described the different birds which made them. The ruddy sheldducks from India made the loudest noise, and it was easy to describe their up and a wigeon whistled gloriously just before the fade-out. So ended our little broadcast, and if the listeners enjoyed it half as much as we did who made it, in its own small way it may have been a success.

I believe it would be possible to convey some of the thrill of wild geese by way of the microphone, and I am anxious to try an outside broadcast from the salt-marshes. It will be very difficult to time, because who knows to the minute when the geese will flight in from the sea?—but with luck on a moonlight night, about the time of high tide, one party of geese might come over during an allotted twenty minutes, and perhaps a curlew or a wigeon would call out and bring variety to the turn.

The music of the geese loses a little, as all music does, in transmission, though perhaps it would lose less over the air than it does when turned into sound track for the films; yet even in the heavy atmosphere of a tiny theatre at a film studio I have been greatly moved by the sound of five hundred pink-footed geese which had passed over a microphone two hundred miles away and two months before.

I have never heard the call of geese on the wireless, though I have imitated it. I began a broadcast, which forms the next chapter and was part of the Empire programme one night in August 1936, by calling:

'Angank—Angank—Angank.'

PINK-FOOTED GEESE, UP UNDER THE SUN *Oil Painting*

WIGEON STANDING IN SHALLOW WATER *Oil Painting 18″ × 15″*

CHAPTER NINE

A BROADCAST

'Angank, Angank.'

'That peculiar noise, which you may have mistaken for atmospherics, was me imitating a wild goose!'

Thus began a broadcast talk which occupied fifteen minutes of the Empire programme one August night in 1936, at what was midnight at home, but all sorts of different hours to the people who may have heard it in far away parts of the world.

I went on to tell of my home and the birds which live there.

'By trade I am a painter. Amongst other things I paint birds, and the sort of birds that I paint most are wild-fowl—ducks and geese and swans and the like. They are the wildest of all birds, and so they live in the wildest parts now left in England, which are the marshy estuaries of our coast. On the lonely wastes of mud and salt marsh they collect in winter in enormous crowds, and so as to be near them I live, and do my painting, in a lighthouse on one of these estuaries on the east coast of England. Some lighthouses have raging seas all round them and some don't. Mine is one of those that don't. It stands on the end of the bank of a river just at its mouth. When the tide is in there is water on three sides, but when the tide is out you can walk for about four miles to seaward, first over salt marsh, then over soft mud, and then over hard yellow sand. And *then* you would only come to a narrow channel of water and after that there would be more sand, some of it stretching out ten miles from the shore—but all covered when the tide comes rushing in as fast in some places as a man can run. In order to have some of the birds that I paint always near, more or less as models, I have enclosed about six acres of the salting round the lighthouse, and in this enclosure I keep lots of tame water-fowl. It is about these, and how they were caught and how I hope to catch more and different kinds, that I want to tell you.

'My birds are mostly pinioned, which means that they cannot fly, but then they do not have to fly to get their food, and they have no enemies to escape, so they really live a very contented life. They grow a little lazy perhaps, but they also grow very tame, and that is one of their greatest charms. In less than a week a goose caught wild will come up and feed with the others within five yards of what was its most deadly enemy—a man. Of course they very soon distinguish between one man and another, and they may be a little shy of strangers although they are perfectly tame with the person who feeds them. Besides their engaging tameness they are also very handsome. Some of them are brilliant in colour and pattern and others have quieter colours but are beautifully trim in shape.

'Most of my geese have been caught in nets at various times, either flight nets or clap nets. The clap nets are the most exciting. Some of them are those that have been wing-tipped when shooting. They recover in a day or two and get just as tame as the netted ones. Some of them breed in captivity, more particularly the ducks than the geese, and rearing the young ones is very difficult, but of course correspondingly fascinating. The most exciting part, however, is the actual catching of the geese. As many wild-fowlers know, it is pretty difficult to outwit wild geese even with a gun, and when it is a matter of catching them alive it is five times as difficult and therefore five times as thrilling. If you are successful you have a bird that will give you infinite pleasure perhaps for years and years. As you watch it feeding at your feet, or preening its feathers or chasing away some unfortunate young gander, you can say to yourself, or better still to some friend, "Now the morning I caught that chap was awfully exciting", and then you can tell the story.

'I went out to Hungary this spring to see the geese which live on a great green plain called the Hortobarge, which is spelt Hortobagy. They come there in countless thousands on migration, and they only stay for about three weeks in the spring before going north to breed. In March there were, I believe, at least a hundred thousand geese. They lived all over the plain in

GOLDEN EAGLE *Oil Painting 24″ × 24″*

RED BREASTED GEESE AND LESSER WHITEFRONT

Oil Painting 8′ × 3′

flocks of between five and ten thousand, so that when they rose they almost darkened the sky. They were mostly white-fronted geese with some of a smaller very beautiful bird, the lesser white-fronted goose, which has only once ever been recorded in England, although they probably come from time to time without being recognised.

'At the end of a week in Hungary I had fifteen live geese, which included one of the lesser white-fronts which had been wounded by a wild-fowler out there. He had a badly broken wing, but we put it in splints made of two pieces of firewood and bandaged it up and then wound the bandage twice right round his body, so as to keep the wing in close to his side. We spent a night in Budapest on the way home and the geese were given a sort of pantry on the third floor of one of the biggest hotels, because I did not at all want to leave them cooped up in their crates all night. Next morning we went on board an aeroplane, geese and all; and the same evening we were in London. The geese roosted that night in our garden in London, which has a little pond in it, and they cleaned themselves up after the journey and had a good meal of wheat, and then next day I took them to the lighthouse by car. They all arrived safely and within about four days they came up to feed with the others almost at my feet. The little lesser white-front had preened himself up so that the bandages round his body were quite hidden in the feathers, and no one would have known that they were there. In Hungary they call lesser white-fronts Kish Lilliks; "kish" being small, and "lillik" because that is the noise they make. I think it is rather a nice name. After about three weeks or so I caught up my kishlillik and cut off all the bandages and splints. The wing was completely mended. I could just feel where the break had been, and now you would never know that he had been wounded at all. He is almost the prettiest of all my geese, because although his chief colour is dark brownish grey, he is beautifully marked and he has smart black bars across his breast. His legs are brilliant orange and his beak is a delicate pink. His forehead is white, which of course is why he is called white-fronted, and he has bright yellow eyelids which make a little yellow ring round each eye. He really is the neatest, most perfect little goose, hardly bigger than a duck. In fact, he is at present the apple of my eye. But there is another even more beautiful kind of wild goose called the red-breasted goose. Its breast is the richest dark chestnut and the rest of it is black and white. The white traces beautiful patterns on its head and neck and sides, separating the red from the black. Red-breasted geese are very rare in England, indeed there are only about a dozen records of them ever having strayed so far west. Their real home in winter is the Caspian Sea, and they breed on marshes at the mouths of the rivers Obi and Yenesei which run into the Arctic Ocean in the very north of Siberia. A few redbreasts come as far west as Hungary in the winter, and when I was there I saw about thirty altogether. It was my first sight of them alive. One morning a big crowd of geese were passing over, just after sunrise—about six or seven hundred of them, and then suddenly I heard a different call note amongst them. Straight overhead were thirteen little geese flying in a bunch with quick wing beats. They were dark and had short necks and white sterns, and every now and then one would turn or twist and show a glint of red in the morning sun. I saw another lot of sixteen redbreasts that day and later I saw several odd ones and a bunch of four.

'But I could not catch any, chiefly because there were not really enough there amongst the countless thousands of white-fronted geese.

'I am determined to get one, however, even if I have to go to the Caspian Sea for it. In fact I have a bet with a friend that within twelve months there will be a red-breasted goose in the pen at my lighthouse. First I shall try Hungary again, and failing that I shall work gradually eastward until I come to the Caspian. There, perhaps on the delta of the Volga, or perhaps in the South Caspian, which is in Persia, I may find a red-breasted goose.

'With any luck I might catch more than one. Three or four pairs I should *like* to bring back. They are terribly rare in captivity, so if one wants to have red-breasted geese walking about in one's garden, there is nothing for it but the Caspian Sea; unless, of course, one was lucky in Hungary, or the Danube delta or the Crimea; but on the whole it would be a pity to be done out of a visit to Astrakhan.

'One of the pink-footed geese in my pen was very lame and eventually his foot had to be amputated. So since he had not the use of his foot I

GEESE MOVING FROM STUBBLE TO POTATOES *Oil Painting 18″ × 15″*

decided to let him have the use of his wings, and this year I let him grow full wings.

'The moult is in July, and then the old flight feathers which had been cut off short were shed and the new perfect ones began to grow. By August they were nearly full length. I was away in Germany at the time, and when I came back, as I drove down the bank towards the lighthouse, I saw a single goose flying far out over the salting. It was Long John Silver in person, my old one-legged goose. He circled in towards home, flew once round the lighthouse, and then swept down and made a perfect landing in the pen.

'The geese will soon be here again, migrating southward from the land of midnight sun. I shall go to Scotland, as I do most years, to meet them in September and watch them arriving, tired and hungry after their long journey, but still the wildest of all wild things, and I shall get as much of a thrill from the sight as I have always got. There will be about five thousand geese on this one special marsh when they have all arrived. Perhaps if it has been a good breeding year in Spitzbergen and Greenland there will be more, and when they rise from the marsh in the evening to fly out to the sand to roost, there will be a roar as of thunder. 'Skein after skein will pass across the sunset, calling in glorious chorus. Those are the moments that I try hard to capture in my paintings.

'If I have been able even to suggest how thrilling it can be, perhaps it will be some sort of explanation of that peculiar madness from which some of us suffer—a desperate longing to be out at dawn on the mudflats with the flood tide rustling past up the creek and the call of wild geese in our ears.'

Brucie shot a bean goose (*segetum* and a pretty large one, too). Home in the dark. The inn is very comfortable with a fine gypsy band at supper and admirable Hungarian food.

'Sun. morn. Up at 3 o'clock and drove seven miles in cart in dark. (Just shot a single goose, my twelfth this morning, and she's only wingtipped, so I'm keeping her in the bottom of my pit.) Anyway, it was a calm morning and all the geese were high. There were about forty or fifty thousand in our vicinity, but being Sun. there were no end of gunners.

'I only fired twenty shots and got seven geese—all whitefronts. A man near me fired over seventy shots and got three! In the early morning there were three lots of five or six lesser whitefronts. They came past low like teal. As teal are to wigeon, so are lesser wfs. to wfs.

'There are, of course, lots of other interesting birds—notably of prey. I saw several white-tailed eagles, a harrier, two rough-legged buzzards and two red-footed falcons (I think, but they might have been merlins), ruffs and spotted shank, wigeon, teal, garganey, mallard, pintail, but ducks are not numerous.

'There were about three lots of greylags during the flight, about twenty or thirty in each, but they are apparently commoner in autumn. There were also quite a lot of beans about. BUT, the *pièce de résistance,* the 'high spot' of the morning—three geese coming low on my right. One of them has a very short neck, it is very dark and small. As it passes there is a flash of chestnut. Eighty yards out and shining in the sun passes the first red-breasted goose I have ever seen alive. There are two lesser whitefronts with him. When he is past I can see that his tummy has much more white than the others—and so he goes off to be swallowed up in ten thousand geese which are sitting three-quarters of a mile away. I'm (blast! my pen's run out—now pencil). I'm sorry about the present tense, etc., but it *was* an event, wasn't it.

'(Between us my live goose and I have made a wretched mess of this paper, because whenever I hear a goose coming the letter gets trodden into the mud! I've just missed an absolute sitter, quite low. It's the third time this morning.)

EVENING ON THE PUZSTA—MARCH *Oil Painting 18″ × 15″*

WHITEFRONTS COURTING *Oil Painting 30″ × 20″*

'We started very early this morning. I've just got another splendid live bird. I must go out and catch it and then I'll tell you about the early morning and two thrills. Well, I'm back again and the score is nineteen, and my pensioner is only just wingtipped, a splendid bird—so back to the early morning.

'We came out to the north from the csarda, and since this wasn't a bit where the fifty thousand had been the day before—at least eight miles from it, in fact—I wasn't very hopeful, but one can't talk to the guides, because they only talk Hungarian, which is impossible, so there was nothing to do but wait and see.

'I was put into a pit by a little pool and there were geese murmuring upwind in a semi-circle. It was a cloudless dawn and cold—thin ice on the splashes. There were a few odd birds about in the dawn. Suddenly there was a noise not only metaphorically but literally like a train. A grey mist appeared just above the horizon and all the geese in creation were in the air. They flew round and settled again. Then there was the same grey mist a mile away on the right and again on the left and then behind me—everywhere except just the track we had driven out along. There were certainly five thousand geese in each "mist" and about five such mists within two miles of me all round, and this eight miles from where the masses all were yesterday. It's pretty safe to say you never see the same geese twice here! If there aren't more than a hundred thousand, there really and truly can't be less.

'They flighted the opposite way from me—mostly, but I had a good flight. Once a pair came past at enormous speed and fairly high, so it seemed. I got the first stony but the other one dived down suddenly and I couldn't even get the second barrel off. I suspected and rushed out. The little bird had a tiny beak and a brilliant yellow ring round its eye—my first lesser whitefront.

'Almost immediately afterwards a big wave of geese came over. High above and behind them I heard a new noise, short but very squeaky, not unlike a wf. but fairly easily distinguishable. By now it was quite light and I grabbed the glasses. Were they? weren't they?—they were—thirteen of them. Rufibranta ruficolis. I didn't see much of the colour, but the shape was more compact and perfect than any other goose.

'A little later I heard the noise again in the distance. It was another little bunch—sixteen redbreasts and one lesser wf. planing down with set wings from a great height. Their flight is almost reminiscent of a golden plover, so short are their necks. The chances of getting one alive are slight, but one *might* get a wingtipped one, and they *would* look nice at the lighthouse.

'Well, I can see the cart coming now, so I'll have to stop. I'll write again in a day or two.

Yours,

Peter.'

EVENING FLIGHT ON THE HUNGARIAN PLAINS

Oil Painting 18″ × 15″

CHAPTER ELEVEN

TO ROUMANIA

IN the autumn of 1936 I went again to the great goose plain of the Hortobagy in Hungary. There was not such a great concentration of geese as I had seen there in the spring. Instead of a hundred thousand whitefronts there were only twenty thousand. There were fewer lesser whitefronts too, than in March, and I saw no red-breasted geese at all.

We stayed there a week shooting a few geese each day and setting up nets to try and catch them alive at night. But there was a moon and we caught none.

So we decided to go further east and see if there were redbreasts to be found at the delta of the Danube on the Black Sea. Accordingly Tony and I took train to Bucharest and then went by car down towards the delta. Our first stop was at Gropeni, a small village just above Braila. Here was a strip of grassy plain about a mile and a half wide which flanked the river, and which was sometimes flooded when the river rose in the spring. At this time of year it was dry except for a number of reedy ponds and a few larger expanses of water, with various channels and creeks leading out of them.

We arrived unfortunately on the very first day of the blizzard which heralded the continental winter.

Our first night was spent in great discomfort in a very primitive house on an island in the Danube, but next day we removed, complete with an army of guides and hangers-on, to the mainland again, and found another tiny house on the outskirts of the village of Gropeni. In this house I wrote of our adventures in a letter to John:

'. . . . We arrived in two cars at the same time as a perishing blizzard, and on the way we stalked about seventy whitefronts sitting near a ditch in the snow, on the edge of a grass marsh which borders the Danube on its west side. It was an easy stalk and we split, and I popped my head up within about ten yards, and being in travelling clothes and therefore cool (it really was perishing, although I admit it's a poorish excuse), I bagged—nothing—except one that fell a half-mile off and we couldn't find because it fell belly up in the snow, and so on with the dance, and over the Danube in a colossal Thames punt, with the most primitive sail. So far from being blue the Danube is the dirtiest brown that you can think of.

'In the evening we went to a deserted pool in a deserted wood where there were said to have been geese. In point of fact I believe a few pairs of grey-lags bred there in the summer! Anyway we saw three ducks and no geese at all. This morning it still snowed and blew, and the army was unwilling to make the sea passage across the Danube in the heavy seas. Actually it was quite rough as the Danube is about three-quarters of a mile wide there and that is only a part of it.

'The result was that we crossed in broad daylight, and since we had no idea in the blizzard where anything was (visibility 200 yards) and since the army had considerably less, sport, as you can imagine, was not brisk. One big lot of geese came over fairly high and Tony bagged one, but I failed to register. I then shot a duck, of which there were quite a few, and saw several white-tailed eagles, and narrowly missed being under several lots of geese, but it was altogether too miserably cold—all clothes frozen stiff, etc. Hands could not remain ungloved—birds frozen solid in a few minutes.

'So we went home and removed to a new village on this side of the Danube, so that the army would not have to come plaintively to us as they did this morning and say, "We have children, we have wives!" Anyhow, it was a shocking place, and I seldom remember to have spent a less comfortable night, having a wretched cold—no hot food at all, lots of mice—we haven't found the lice yet but expect them daily.

SHOVELERS AT 9 O'CLOCK *Oil Painting 24" × 24"*

TEN LITTLE REDBREASTS *Oil Painting 30" × 25"*

'Here however it is more comfortable. This afternoon we went out in a sleigh, still perishing wind, but not actually snowing. We saw a tremendous lot of teal sitting (no doubt owing to the weather) as I've never yet seen teal sit, in bunches so tight that you couldn't believe they were birds, all along the edge of some enormous pools. We saw a peregrine take a pigeon from near the village. He looked grand lit up from below by the snow. Tony saw him actually grab: I only saw him carrying the parti-coloured pigeon.

'We tried stalking the geese with one of our sleigh horses, because we had an assinine man with us who had spent the previous night telling us that it was the only known method of shooting geese. Doubtless he had seen it successfully done, but, as I had expected, it was a case of once bit twice shy, for they got up at 150 yards. Ducks were very little tamer. Later the expedition developed into a round tour to see what we could see. First we saw about 100 or more greylags sheltering in some reeds with some mallards (altogether two or three thousand I should think). Then we saw about 600 whitefronts sitting so thick that one couldn't believe they were geese, mostly lying down and feeding, so as to keep out of the wind.

'I looked at them with the glass, but it was hard to make them out, as they all looked black in the snow and there was a mist of powdered snow blowing past in front of them, but suddenly I saw some white streaks and there they were, seven little redbreasts. Part of the flock moved and when they settled again they were further away and there were twelve redbreasts, and still two stayed with the near lot. We walked fairly close, but it was too cold to hold the glasses up for long. I tried with the horse again, but they got up at at least 100 yards. As we left I took a last look at them over on the far grass where they had settled (a place where the wind had blown the snow mostly away). They all turned and walked down wind picking their way amongst the whitefronts—fourteen little redbreasts all in a row.

'After that we saw about 1500 more whitefronts, but not to peruse in detail, and quite a lot of distant geese (a woman has just brought in the dirtiest jug of water I have *ever* seen—not only is the water dull mud colour but the jug itself is covered with large splashes of congealed gravy and the eleven kilometres home and the road so full of snowdrifts that we had to go over the fields and we had to walk through snow a foot deep mostly, because the horses couldn't pull the sleigh *and* us. It took us about two and a half hours and was dark about half way. We'd been about sixteen miles and seen about one hundred geese, and one other nice thing, just before we got to the far village—six great birds, slow flapping and high in the air, lit from below by the snow and looking very pale—bustards. Added to these we must have seen about fifteen whitetailed eagles, a merlin, a rough-legged buzzard, and a kite. One of our army has just come in to say he found a goose eaten by an eagle. We drew a map and he pointed to the place and it was *identically* the place where Tony's bean goose had fallen the second time.

'The snow has driven the geese away so much that tomorrow we are off—Tony home, as he has to be in London by Tuesday, and I further down the delta to see what is to be seen down there.'

FOUR REEDS

Oil Painting 18″ × 15″

PINTAILS DOWN WIND *Oil Painting 18″ × 15″*

CHAPTER TWELVE

THE DELTA AND THE BLACK SEA

'Started in a steamer between Tulcea and Valcov on the Danube—not so truly blue.'

'My Dear John,

Things haven't got much brighter lately. The snow has pretty well spoiled everything. I packed off Tony to London (according to previous arrangement) about two days ago from Braila, which is a truly miserable spot, especially in a snowstorm. I went to the pictures and saw Mr. Warner Oland in a Charlie Chan film, and Elizabeth in "As you like it". Then at seven a.m. next morning, in a wretched snowstorm, I made the discovery that my Leica had been stolen. I have an Insurance taken out in Debrecen, so they may ?? pay me for it. Anyway it wasn't too bright a start to a ship journey, which I had postponed till the morning so as to see the country. Visibility was about three hundred yards most of the time. I saw six hundred geese in one place. Arrived at Tulcea, I went to call on Dr. Rettig, whom I knew by name as the local ornithologist. He was charming, and a good taxidermist. He had stuffed two redbreasts, but said that only four had ever been shot in the Delta, which was not encouraging. Of course, he didn't believe I had seen fourteen at Gropeni, nor would he believe that we had shot two bean geese, because I had given the corpses to the British Consul at Braila, and the bean goose is not recorded from the Delta. I had brought the two lesser whitefronts for him, as I expected he might not have a young one. Anyway, he hadn't any at all, so was quite pleased, but would have preferred the beans. We went to the cinema together and saw

THE COMING OF WINTER ON THE DANUBE DELTA

Oil Painting 60" × 40"

"La Cucaracha" and "The Last Days of Pompeii", and then I went back and had supper with him. He warmed up and eventually accepted my bean geese *and* my redbreasts.

'At about midday we embarked on this little ship. The point is that there are known to be geese at or near Babadag, and believed to be geese at or near Valcov (which is pronounced Vallcough—to rhyme with Hall-cough—and which is also where caviar is caught!).

'Well, the snow is such that the thirty-five kilometres from Tulcea to Babadag could only be traversed in a sleigh or wagon, taking eight hours, whereas in a day or two it may be passable to autos if the snow goes on melting as fast as it is now. So the plan is to go by boat (which doesn't mind if it snows ink—much) and then, if that is no good, come back, by which time the road may be clear. So that is what we are now doing, Herr Lautner (my trusty guide) and I. On the way we have seen three lots of geese, about one hundred in each, and a good many ducks roosting afloat in the Danube. One lot only got up when the boat was about fifteen yards from them. I have seen some kites and a good many eagles and buzzards (rough-legged) and peregrines, and a very pale grey harrier which I think must be a pallid harrier. Teal and wigeon fairly common—one pintail drake. Anyway, there should be plenty of pelicans at Valcov, and I shall be quite amused to see them.

'The snow has been wretched bad luck, as up till then there really must have been a lot of geese. All are agreed that they blackened and deafened respectively the sky and the ear!

'Herr Lautner has just come to say that the Crystal Palace is burnt down; poor old Crystal Palace!

'The engines have stopped so I suppose that means we're there—if only ten thousand geese are too, all will be well.

'Seven-thirty p.m. Three-quarters of an hour later. It seems as though they may be. We have arrived, installed our baggage in a less verminous-looking house than usual, and I am now sitting in a nice little wine house (they don't have any beer here) surrounded by staring small boys, and eating chicken and rice. Near at hand is Herr Lautner cross-questioning all the fishermen, and from the frequence of the word "göshti", I believe we've found some geese at last.

'The people here mostly talk Russian. Quite a lot of them have snow on their boots! They sing, which is quite merry of them, but I do wish they didn't eat garlic. Also, they all play backgammon.

'Here are some miscellaneous facts about Roumania in general:

'There are lots of wolves. They ate six sheep at Gropeni the night before we left.

'Hoodie crows are the commonest bird and take the place of sparrows in the villages. Rooks and jackdaws also live in the villages and towns, feeding in the streets. The only kind of sparrows I have seen are tree sparrows. I've also seen goldfinches and any amount of crested larks.

'We all but got arrested at Gropeni because we went out without Herr Lautner and were unable to explain that our innumerable papers were at home.

'A census of verminous insects in Roumania would look like elaborate astronomical data, whilst the insects themselves would, I am sure, if placed end to end, easily reach from here to the moon!

'I am permitted, by special dispensation, to catch alive in nets "two pieces of each sorts of birds except swans and eagles".

'Here one can eat caviar with a tablespoon (only I haven't done so yet because I haven't been here long enough).

'I am now in Bessarabia—so what do you think of that?

'A shootist told me he had shot seventy-eight swans at one flight—"vive le sport".

'I wish Herr Lautner would come back as I want to hear the news. But he's gone off to see the chief commissar of the hunting!

'The ill-omened man has come back with the news that we're not allowed to hunt here at all. He is now arguing with the gentry all round, but it appears that we may have some bother whatever they say. However, with any luck we can arrange things on the telephone.

'Since when he has been talking earnestly with an unshaven gentleman in the corner. I took him to be perhaps the local taxi driver with whom

FOUR TEAL *Oil Painting 30″ × 25″*

TEAL IN THE AFTERNOON *Oil Painting 30″ × 20″*

he was bargaining to take us out, but he turned out to be the chief of police. First of all I found that shooting was not permitted within one-and-a-half kilometres of the frontier, then I found that tomorrow is a public holiday when no shooting is permitted, but after that we can go where we please—the chief of police says so! So tomorrow I shall go round with a glass and see as much of the place as I can.

* * * * *

'Twenty-four hours later and I sit again in the same little wine house. Apparently all last night's difficulties were satisfactorily overcome, as we took a gun with us and found no one to say us nay.

'This town is a sort of Venice, full of canals, and it is also full of frontier outposts—soldiers, etc. Anyway we left at an unpunctual five from a canal outside our very door in a sort of coble—a large black boat with peaked ends rowed by two lusty young fishermen. It was a big boat, about thirty feet long, so as to brave the perils of the ocean.

'After rowing I should say about three hours—eighteen kilometres, down a widish arm of the river flanked with reeds, we came to the Black Sea—only it was an ugly yellowish grey as it was blowing quite hard. There were hundreds of small boats fishing for sturgeons (actually about thirty, but they were all in a bunch and they looked a lot).

'We turned north and went along the shore. The sea was quite calm as the wind was off the shore. The shore itself was reeds, colossal reeds. These delta reeds are something special. They are almost all fifteen feet high. I measured one of eighteen feet; and they are said to grow to over twenty feet in places. The water was very shallow near the edge (there are no tides) and presently we came round a corner and saw a very marvellous sight. There was an enormous bay, perhaps two miles across, and parts of it were shallow, with grey sandbars showing. There were masses of ducks, and there in the middle, and quite near, was a great flock of whoopers. There were seventy-five of them, a few young ones, but mostly white. They made a tremendous noise when we put them up. By now we were sailing and going fairly fast, so we got quite close. They got up and settled at the back of the bay with some more. I counted one hundred and seventeen in that lot with about sixty greylags amongst them. The ducks were mainly mallards and teal, but after that gadwall were the commonest. I saw dozens and dozens of them. There were shovelers and wigeon and three pintail drakes (presumably with their ducks) and shelducks, and about a dozen pochards and later four tufted ducks, and a pair of goosanders, and overhead was a whitetailed eagle and at the back, over the reeds, were two species of harrier and rough-legged buzzards. There were about ten thousand ducks, and then further on on another spit were eighty more swans and about one thousand geese—all greylags to a bird. Some of the ducks were in shallow water and amongst them were two gulls—but even gulls in these parts might be interesting, I thought, so I looked at them with the glasses. They were avocets. Beyond were curlews. We passed the geese and came to a little fishing hut. There were four men preparing sturgeon lines. They catch them with a sort of spiller—a line with bare hooks (very large) hanging on short strings every foot or two along it. The hooks aren't baited at all, the principle being that the fish just runs into it by accident. It is attached to floats so that when one hook catches hold, the others coil round and also catch in the sturgeon and he's soon "taffled up small". They only catch four or five in a year, each fisher, but they fetch about £30 each or more.

'We sailed on northward and saw two drake goosanders shining in the sun, and about three hundred more geese, all 'lags again. They were all sleeping on the sand and clearly must have been feeding at night under the moon. But where do they feed? Local legend has it that they don't fly at all, but subsist on a kind of aquatic nut which grows in these parts, and is rather larger than a walnut, only with sharp spikes all over it. That I believe to be an old wives' tale. That leaves two possible explanations—one, that grass did grow on the sandbanks until the recent storms in which eight ships were sunk in the Black Sea (which is what the people say), and two, that somewhere inland from the reeds there is a feeding place for the geese. This last theory was backed up on the way home, when we saw three or four lots of 'lags going inland at colossal height in a northwesterly direction.

'We managed to stalk and walk up several ducks and teal on the way home and the total bag was five mallards and four teal.

'I think it is likely that I shall go away again, as the main point is the redbreasts and there aren't any with the 'lags—and time is getting short and I like seeing as much as possible now that I am here. I shall probably go down to Babadag if the snow permits.

'I may go shooting with the chief of police tomorrow, but I doubt it, and now, if I don't stop writing, I shall fall asleep where I sit, which will be a treat for my fellow diners. So good-night.'

CHAPTER THIRTEEN

THE RETURN JOURNEY

Hortobagyicsarda,
Hungary.

'My Dear John,

Here I am back again and sitting in the csarda bar (because the season is really finished and the dining-room is closed down) and the time is about five p.m., and I've just shot three geese and two ducks—but there is quite a lot to tell before that. The story is chiefly of entomological interest. Having travelled a good bit in Roumania I really must have improved the breeding stock of the vermin herds tremendously by the introduction of fresh blood into each neighbourhood.

'After posting the letter to you on the ship and eating a teal which we had cooked for lunch, we went ashore at Tulcea at about midday and found that the snow was still blocking the road to Babadag, which you may remember is in the southern part of the Danube delta, to the exclusion of autos, and so the only way was five hours in a cart: and what a cart! I consider that five hours to be about as uncomfortable as any five hours of transit I have ever spent. As Herr Lautner remarked ten minutes after we started—it was enough to rattle the eyes out of one's head—and it went on for more than thirty kilometres. We passed over some fairly high hills with six foot snowdrifts still uncleared on the road. We had to go round them over the fields, which was the only comfortable part of the journey. There were the remains of war trenches still all along the road. Well, at the end we came to a marshy valley at the head of Lacul Babadag, which is quite a big lake. It was mostly frozen up at the top end, with big islands of high reeds and several hundred ducks sitting on the ice. In one place were about forty greylags sitting in the water. It was getting dark, but by the time we

GREYLAGS ALIGHTING

Oil Painting 30″ × 20″

had found a house in the village of Zebil in which to live, it was already too dark to be worth flighting. And what a house when we did find it! One old man lived there with his son and would be glad to put us up if we had some tobacco for him. He had only one room—it was in fact the house. The room had a big square stove of mud in the corner (as all houses in these parts do), and from it one half of the room was raised about eighteen inches like a sort of stage. Admirable for charades, but less attractive as a bed (with one big quilted blanket) for myself, Herr Lautner, the old man *and* his son. After supping off a little black bread and some pickled water melon it was time for bed. With the utmost difficulty I managed to prepare a jersey to cover the pillow without giving offence and eventually we all lay down in a row. Having always learnt that a flea was remarkable in that it could jump one hundred times its own height, comparable to a man jumping as high as the Eiffel Tower, I spent some time idly speculating on the precise height of a flea. But before very long it became painfully apparent that there was not room on the shelf for the four of us to be out of hopping range—so that was that.

'Nobody could call me fussy—and I hadn't had any clothes off at all for over a week (the principle being that they had more trouble getting through if one kept well battened down), but I must say I found that night uncomfortable. Next morning Herr Lautner and I went out early, but we saw very little except for a fox running across the ice and some ducks in the open water in the middle and the forty geese which we walked into feeding on the shore of the lake. We heard quite a big lot of greylags over the other side of the lake.

'We went back to a splendid breakfast of what remained of last night's black bread, still on the table and a good bit staler than it had been: and since it had begun to snow again I decided to quit. There's no doubt the geese *had* been there. One or two fields I walked over which were clear of snow were absolutely smothered in droppings. But I was fed up with being always too late.

'We ordered a waggon to take us to Babadag. On the way we drove over a causeway. There were waggons and people going along this causeway all the time, but the ducks were crossing it—flying into the snowstorm only about twenty feet up—and streaming across. And so were a good many 'lags—a bit higher, but not much. Further on I suddenly saw a single whitefront sitting in a field. I managed to stalk it under cover of a bank and brought it to bag. Then we saw four hundred 'lags sitting in a bay and, as we watched, a lot came in and settled on the grass quite near us, and a flight began. The flight passed over a reed bed and I was sure I could get under it unseen, and even if the flight was finished by the time I got there I would be in direct line if they were put up, and so close that they would be sure to pass over me. I was quite keen to shoot a greylag to see if it had an orange or a pink bill (western or eastern race). However, the fates (I won't grace them with a capital letter—the old wretches) were against me. I was all but there, and the bunches were still swinging in over the reeds one hundred and fifty yards in front of me, when a blessed cart must needs go trundling past and out went all the geese, passing only just out of shot. I waited for a while but they didn't come back, in spite of an eagle which tried to help. It drove some geese and ducks towards me, but the geese turned off. I could have shot the ducks but still hoped the geese would flight in again. As it turned out they flitted the other way across the lake, and so we went on and caught the train at Babadag and were in Bucuresti (Bucharest) at eleven and I went, just as I was—rubber boots, four or five days' beard and a fortnight's fleas—to the best hotel, the Splendid Park.

'Next morning I took a census of insect bites, but after counting three hundred I gave it up. Later in the day (after hearing news of the constitutional crisis) I took train to Puspokladany (if you can do that one first go off you're cleverer than I thought you were!) and thence to Debrecen. I had an amusing time at the frontier. I had lost my import permits for the guns, including Tony's, which he had left in Bucuresti for me to bring, and I had a rather wretched time wondering what line I would take when I got to the frontier. On the Roumanian border they opened a suitcase and I found my permits and so felt quite happy again, but at the Hungarian Customs they never asked for the permit anyway, indeed they never even noticed that I had two guns, so all the worry for nothing. I got to Debrecen

WIGEON ON A WINDY AFTERNOON *Oil Painting 10″ × 7″*

CONVERSATION PIECE

Oil Painting 30" × 20"

at five o'clock this morning and slept at the Queen of England Hotel until eight-thirty, and then old Nemeth drove me out to the csarda and so here I am. There is a little snow on the puzta and all the water is well frozen. The report was no geese and very few ducks. This afternoon I walked round the new reservoir. Underneath the pumping station was open water and Istvan said there might be some ducks. There were, and I shot a right and left of them as they rose from under the sluice. One of them had a fish in its mouth of the perch tribe, about four inches long, and it was still alive when Istvan picked the duck up. He threw the fish back into the water and it swam off!

'There was a little patch of open water on the reservoir, and about one hundred and fifty ducks where there had been twenty thousand. But, although it's disappointing to see the place bare of birds, there's something rather awe-inspiring about the continental winter and the way it has come down with a north wind driving all before it.

'However, having heard about the absence of geese, I was surprised to hear a roar over Borsus, and presently the first waves of birds arrived to roost on the ice of the reservoir. I couldn't get rid of Istvan and, since I was in white and he in black, he was a considerable handicap in the snow. The geese kept swerving off and also it was pretty dark. That is to account for the fact that I fired about sixteen shots and only collected three geese. Two others slanted out on to the ice and we ought to get at least one of them in the morning—if the eagles don't get them first. Altogether at least two thousand geese came to roost from Borsus, but they say that there are more at Holaskus, so I shall go there in the morning although it's much further.

'I have to wait here until Wednesday because I can't get permits for the live geese before then. Nemeth Ur has sent away to the next village, ten miles away, for my favourite gypsy violinist, and he has just arrived by the train and is now playing "Nem tudom ehn mivon vellem". This really is rather a sweet place. Everyone treats one as if one had come home. Tremendous welcomes. When we left for Roumania a fortnight ago the gypsies brought their instruments out and played us into the car and away! And now they are playing my favorite tunes in honour of my return, including one they have composed about "Scott Peter" and his hunt for "vörös nyaku liba" (Red-necked geese).

'The live geese are rather exciting. Since I have been away they have collected quite a lot. So far the nets have not caught anything, but the moon has a lot to do with that. But the pen contains sixteen geese—eleven whitefronts, one bean, and four kish lilliks—and on Thursday I shall set off for England with them all.'

* * * * *

And on Thursday I did set off with the live geese in three large crates. At Budapest they were loaded into an aeroplane and we flew to Vienna. At Vienna there were reports of bad weather and fog ahead. I and the geese were the only passengers and the pilot told me that if the fog were bad we would not stop at Prague but go straight on to Leipzig.

But the fog was bad at Leipzig too, and we had not enough petrol to go on. We came down gingerly, dropping into the grey blanket of fog, saw a chimney-top flash by, and zoomed up again into the sunshine. Three times we tried unsuccessfully to get down, and then flew a few miles to a military airport at Erfurt where we found, as the wireless had reported, a thin patch in the mist and we landed safely. We refuelled there with four hundred gallons poured from tins, and then we took off again and flew to Cologne.

At Cologne the service was suspended. England was enshrouded in fog. There had been a bad accident at Croydon, with the loss of fourteen lives that morning, and the geese and I could go no further by air. There was a chance, they said, that I might catch the boat train to the Hook and be in London the next morning; and I was anxious to do this because the crates were small and the geese unfed, for I had been counting on a short journey. But I had so arranged my affairs that I had only just enough money for my taxi in London, so that I might obviate the currency restrictions on the journey across Europe. By the time that the airline had refunded the exact railway fare necessary there was hardly time to catch the train. The bus hurtled from the airport to the station to the great discomfort of

RESPONSIBILITIES *Oil Painting 15″ × 18″*

the other travellers, and accompanied by two airline porters I dashed in to buy my ticket. One of them, carrying my baggage, came with me, whilst the other took charge of the geese.

'You have luggage to register?' asked the booking clerk. 'Then you will have to pay extra for it.' 'Yes,' said I, 'but my train is due to leave, I will have to pay on the train.'

'You must pay now.'

'I have no more money,' I replied, and threw down a few pfennigs which was all that I had. The porter pulled me by the arm. 'Never mind him,' he said, and we dashed up the steps on to the platform.

There was a train moving past the platform at a good speed. The other porter ran up. 'Your geese are in there—in the front van,' he shouted, and I could see that there was not a chance of loading my baggage on to that fast-moving train. But the geese were going to the Hook: baggage or no baggage I must go with them. So I leapt on to the running board, shouted back to the porter, who said, 'All right, I'll send them after you', and pulled myself up into the train.

Once inside I took stock of my position. All that I had with me was a Hungarian fur-collared overcoat, a volume of short stories by Somerset Maugham, and a cheque book. I had no money and I had had no food since a roll at Vienna at ten in the morning. As I walked along the train and through the dining-car I was tortured by the smell of the dinner which my fellow travellers were already enjoying.

I appealed to the head waiter of the dining-car, but he had no suggestions to offer.

When you are hungry it is bad to think about food. I went and sat in a carriage further up the train and thought about food for half an hour. I had just started to think of something else when the little bell sounded in the corridor and the attendant announced the second service. A few moments later an official came to inspect my passport.

'Are there any English people on the train?' I asked him.

'Yes, there are one or two.'

'Which of them would be most likely to lend me a pound?' and I tried hard to look as though I were not a 'confidence man'. But he looked so suspicious that I had to tell him my story and when he admitted that he had heard the geese honk as he passed through the luggage van I knew that I could count on his support.

He led me to a benevolent-looking Englishman who, when I had told my story over again, willingly cashed a cheque for me, and ten minutes later I was eating a hearty dinner.

From then onwards the journey went smoothly enough and by the following evening we had all arrived safely at the lighthouse—eleven whitefronts, four lesser whitefronts, one bean goose and I.

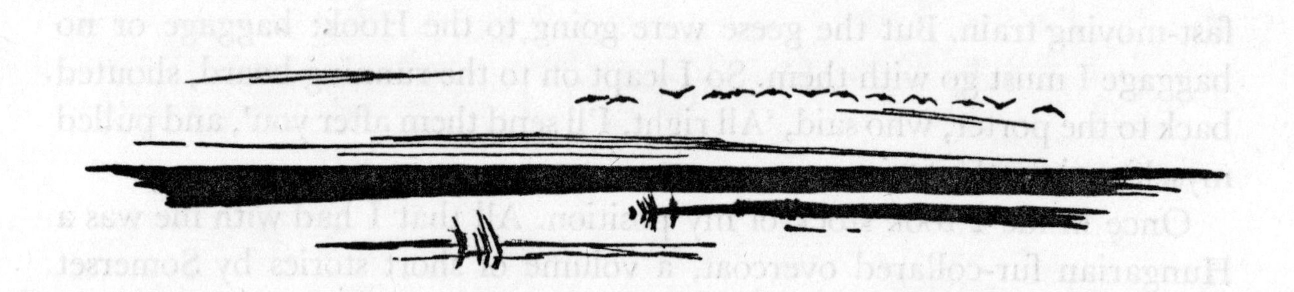

CHAPTER FOURTEEN

THE LESSER WHITEFRONTS

PERSIAN TRAVEL

FAR out in the Transcaspian Steppe in northern Persia we found Atagel, in a hollow behind a low ridge. As we topped the crest, it lay below us, a shallow lake, brilliant blue in the pale sunlight of a winter's afternoon.

The surface of the water was dotted with birds, white dots and black dots and, near by, piebald dots which were shelducks up-ending close to the flat sandy shore. A little row of large and very white dots was a party of pelicans fishing out in the middle. The pink of their plumage made them look whiter than white, but at that distance not pink at all.

There was a family of whooper swans, two white and three grey; and then there were the ducks. They were mostly at the far side, where a little sluggish stream spread out into a marshy delta at the edge of the lake. Wigeon and teal were there in great packs, and there were gadwall and shovelers and red-crested pochards and smews.

Over the flat marsh flew a little party of greylag geese; but standing in the shallows at the edge of the open water was a much more exciting little dark line of birds. They were larger than the surrounding ducks and smaller than the greylags, and most of them were asleep.

I had come three thousand miles to find red-breasted geese, and here, less than a mile away, were fifty sleeping dots that were about the right size, yet too far to show any colour.

Then, as I sat gazing through the telescope, I heard, very dimly at first, the call of geese flying high somewhere away to the northward; it was the high, thin call of lesser white-fronted geese. Presently they came into sight, two hundred strong, flying in a magnificent V. When they saw Atagel they set their wings and started to glide. A fresh burst of calling came across the water and in that instant I knew that I had still to find the haunt of the elusive redbreasts, for they have quite a different, high-pitched barking call. The answer from the water was lesser whitefront language.

The formation broke, and some of the geese circled back and round, losing height. But most of them flew on, re-forming again, past us, and away south-westwards to the Caspian Sea. Their chorus had died away in the distance by the time that the two small parties, which had broken away and circled downwards, finally joined the flock which stood in the shallows.

I sat for a long time wondering at the vastness of what I had seen. Behind me were the mountains of Persia, a snow-capped frieze stretching across the southern horizon. Somewhere between me and the mountains, in the corner of the Caspian Sea, was their journey's end, the southern limit of migration of the lesser whitefronts. In front lay the steppe whence they had come, unending dry grassy plains stretching away and away to Bokhara and Samarkand.

From their breeding grounds north of the tree line, two thousand miles away, they had come southwards, perhaps following the side of the Ural range, or perhaps the great River Obi, the Irtish, the Tobol, and then striking across the Kirgiz Plain to the Aral Sea.

From there they had come yet farther south, stopping here and there at some lake or river marsh on the way. Atagel was one of those stopping places, and I had seen some of them on the last stage of the great journey.

I followed that south-going skein towards the mountains, and, after hunting for a week, I found at last the lagoon where all the lesser white-fronted geese of the Caspian Sea collect in mid-winter.

From the foothills and the woods I rode out on to the marsh with a high heart. One of the great goose marshes of the world was before me, and far out at the edge of the lagoon smoky clouds of geese rose, circled shimmering in the mirage, and settled again in untold thousands; and a distant murmur like the high singing of gnats came in from the shore.

The horses' hoofs splashed in the pools and puddles, and the grass was gloriously green. Snipe jumped up in front of us, and an occasional pair of mallards clattered out of the rushes. Beyond a belt of dark green rushes were the nearest geese. I went forward on foot and then stalked to the edge of the rushes. There were about three thousand on the short grass before me, and many more stretching away into the rushes beyond, and every one that I could see was a lesser white-fronted. Surely these exquisite and delicate little birds, with their golden ringed eyes, their tiny pink bills and smart white foreheads, their brilliant orange legs and black barred tummies, deserve a more romantic name. The Persian 'goz siah kuchik' means 'little black goose', to distinguish it from 'goz sefid'—'white goose'—applied to the greylag. These names serve well enough in a land where the snow goose and the brent are unknown.

The natives of the near-by village of Kara Tappeh knew the red-breasted goose, but only as an occasional visitor in small bunches among the hordes of lesser whitefronts. They called it 'Shahpasand goz', meaning literally 'worthy of the Shah', or, perhaps, 'Royal goose'.

'Kara Tappeh' means 'a black hillock', and the village stands proudly on the little mound in the middle of the marsh, with a characteristic wide-eaved house silhouetted on its very summit.

I stayed there in the house of the head man for a week, wandering on the great marsh. It is about two miles wide between the lagoon and the woods, which are full of enormous boars; tigers roam in these woods, and there are wild pheasants and porcupines. The marsh is about ten miles long, and on it there cannot have been fewer than thirty thousand lesser whitefronts, and I think there were twice as many.

Morning flight was always late, usually just after sunrise, and for half an hour the air was a network of skeins coming in high from the lagoon. As far as I could see in both directions were more and yet more, into the far distance. The black lines on the mud flats became gradually thinner until finally no geese were left at all. Out beyond where they had been the sun lit up the vast crowds of flamingos, and the mirage made them into a rectangular coral pink bar of amazing brilliance.

Behind, over the marsh the geese were flying about in little parties. Occasionally whole masses would rise, disturbed by a shepherd or an eagle or a gyrfalcon, and then settle again like a grey carpet.

I saw no red-breasted geese in the week that I was there, but I learnt the innermost thoughts of the lesser whitefronts on the green marsh at the foot of the snow mountains. It is a wild setting for a wild wild-goose.

FLAMINGOS *Water Colour Drawing 6" × 3"*

CATCHING DUCKS AT NIGHT WITH A FLARE ON A CASPIAN LAGOON *Oil Painting 18″ × 15″*

CHAPTER FIFTEEN

A FLARE, A GONG AND A NET

SIAH DERVESHAN is a typical Caspian village of thatched-roofed cottages built upon the bank of a river in the middle of the great rice swamps of North Persia.

I came to it on a February afternoon, and I liked it so much that I stayed for a fortnight.

We had come by boat from the port of Pahlevi, and we were exploring the great lagoon, searching for red-breasted geese. We had been round the western end of the lagoon, rowing in and out of reed-fringed bays amongst pelicans, flamingos, cormorants, swans, and a host of smaller waterfowl, but the only geese that were to be seen were greylags and whitefronts. We travelled in two small bright blue row boats, in one of which were supplies and baggage, and in the other myself and my faithful Ismail, a Persian youth who spoke a few words of German, and who was, therefore, my interpreter. To propel these vessels came three sturdy boatmen.

It was on the third day that we came to the bay of the 'pig-puddles'. A kind of reedy grass had once grown in the bay, and this had been completely ploughed up by the snouts of wild pigs. There were perhaps two or three hundred acres of this grass, and not one square yard but had been turned over and laid flat by the pigs. The whole bay consisted of little puddles bounded by rolls of matted reed. In the puddles floated little brown seeds and to eat these seeds came thousands of ducks. It was a daylight feeding place, for at night it was almost deserted; but when we first came to the place at about noon there were perhaps fifteen thousand waterfowl in the bay. Mallards and pintails were there in equal numbers, with a sprinkling of other surface-feeding ducks, and amongst them a crowd of geese too. There were greylags and white-fronted, but none of the red-breasted geese for which I sought. Out on the open water of the lagoon were seventy Bewick's swans, and farther out still a party of whoopers. Away to the left sat a shimmering pink line of pelicans on a point of mud. The sun shone out of a clear sky and the trees across the bay were magnified by the mirage.

Behind the bay of pig-puddles was a forest of alders and willows and reeds. Parts of it were swampy and I was told that in these swamps wild ducks were caught at night by strange means; so I decided that this would be a good place to stay for a few days to investigate the stories I had heard.

Half a mile to the eastward was a little river, and a fisherman, whose boat was beached there, told us that there was a village hidden in the trees and that its name was Siah Derveshan.

I walked up a footpath which followed the bank of the river, here and there cutting off a corner and striking across meadowy park land. Ismail came with me and the boats came after us following the lazy curves of the river.

About a mile from the lagoon the land had imperceptibly risen, so that the river on our left was running between steep banks ten feet below us. On our right the woods were flooded and we could hear mallards and teal calling and occasionally see some of them in the few open patches of water that we passed.

Round the corner of the woods we came upon the thatched roofs of the village clustered around the fish trap which spanned the river.

In the village was a small bazaar round a closed courtyard. We entered by one gate and I suggested to Ismail that we should find the head man of the village and ask him if he knew of a house in which we could stay. But Ismail, who was only twenty and shy of disposition, was disinclined to embark upon this self-invitation. I suggested that we might ask for the owner of the nearest *Murdab*. *Murd* means dead and *ab* means water, and this was the name used for the swamps in which I had heard that the ducks were caught by using a flare at night. Under pressure, Ismail made inquiries, and ten minutes later, as I had expected, we were being led off up the river

ESSER WHITE-FRONTS FLIGHTING ALONG THE OPEN LAGOON *Oil Painting 30" × 20"*

bank to the house of the chief duck-catcher, who told us that we might stay with him as long as we liked.

It was a lovely two-storey house with a wide-eaved thatch covering a wooden balcony, and our room was the one in which our host dried his tobacco crop. It had more windows than most Persian rooms, many of which, indeed, have none, and round the walls were neatly stacked bundles of tobacco leaves, for, as duck-catching was his winter livelihood, so tobacco-growing provided his summer income. There was no furniture in the room except a fine carpet and a little brazier of charcoal which was brought in soon after our arrival. Sitting, eating and sleeping are all done at floor level in Persia.

At dusk I was led down through the village again and along the river bank. After half a mile we branched off a few yards into the wood and came, all at once, upon a boat lying in a narrow ditch. It was a tiny flat-bottomed craft with a peaked bow and stern, no more than 12 feet long and 2½ feet wide, and when we embarked there seemed to be horribly little freeboard. Propelling the punt by pole, my guide pushed along the ditch for fifty yards and then turned into another ditch which led at once to a small thatched mud hut. Here there was another punt with a strange curved hood over the bows like the hood of a cobra. In the hut were three more men, one of them our host, the chief duck-catcher or *murdabchi*.

We waited for darkness sitting around a wood fire in the middle of the hut. There was no chimney and the place was full of smoke.

Some time before I had heard about the method which the Caspian duck-catchers used; how they went forth at night with a flare and a gong and could pick the ducks up by hand or catch them with a butterfly net. I had not been able to believe all that I had heard, but how much of it was true I felt I should very shortly know, and as I sat waiting my excitement grew. So it was with a thrill of anticipation that I emerged from the four-foot-high door of the hut an hour later, my eyes streaming from the effects of the wood smoke. One of the men who followed me carried a small brass gong, hanging from an inverted L-shaped stick, in one hand, and a gong stick, padded with flax, in the other.

Outside the hut, by the light of a flaming torch, I could see two large hand nets leaning against the roof. They were about 12 feet long and only about 2½ feet wide. Seven feet of their length was net, bounded by curved willow poles, and the other five feet was handle. At the tip the willow poles were drawn together by a string till their ends were only a foot apart. The net was of very small mesh, so that a sixpenny bit would hardly have passed through it.

One of these nets was selected by the *murdabchi* and I handled it for a moment. So beautifully was it balanced that it seemed to have practically no weight at all.

A small earthenware bowl was brought out of the hut, containing a strange concoction which I learned was bullrush fluff soaked in paraffin, the fuel of the flare. A little lump of it was lit from the torch and placed on an earthen platform on the very bows of one of the punts beneath the hood. This hood, made of reed matting, was about two feet high, built up behind and over the flare to make a shadow, and the *murdabchi*, armed with the net, took his place standing immediately behind it. A place was made for me to sit in the middle of the boat and one of the others climbed into the stern with a pole and pushed off along the narrow ditch. Closely following came the second boat, poled curiously enough from the bows, with the gong-beater in the stern.

Almost as soon as we left the hut the gonging began, at first softly, then gradually rising to a high crashing ring which drowned all other sounds of our progress. For the next half-hour the gong rang thus, rising and falling in intensity by reason more, it seemed, of its strange harmonics than of any intended variation on the part of the ringer.

The punts drove forward at a good speed along a narrow, winding path cut through the reeds and bushes. A mallard rose about five yards away, the splash faintly audible above the ring of the gong; it hung for a moment looking pale yellow in the light of the flare and then disappeared into the darkness.

Suddenly we came upon a pair of mallards sitting in the water half under a willow bush. The boat swung towards them as they swam out into the

PINKFEET SWINGING IN

Oil Painting 30″ × 20″

open. For a moment they paused and then rose. The net came sweeping across and the drake was taken six feet in the air. The net was held upright and the bird fell down into the pocket near the handle whence the catcher removed him, locked his wings and dropped him into the boat. The whole performance was accomplished with a speed and perfection which could only have been born of long practice. The punts never stopped or even slowed up, but swept on along the narrow waterway, propelled with absolute precision round sharp bends, under overhanging branches and through narrow gaps in the great reed beds. A teal jumped from thick rushes on one side and was caught right at the top of the net; another mallard splashed up from a clump of dead docks and was caught by a lightning stroke. A gadwall swam out from the reeds straight ahead, so close that as he rose he was taken in the pocket of the net right against the handle. Many would jump just out of range of the net. The catcher knew exactly when they could not be reached and stood perfectly still, making no attempt unless he were sure of a catch.

Sometimes teal and even the larger ducks would swim away low in the water, trying to hide. If they came out into an open place it was possible, by a special stroke of the net, to scoop them out of the water, but there was a much better method. The catcher would squeak by sucking through his lips, as if he were calling to a dog, and the sound was apparently audible to the duck above the din of the gong. This would make the most unwilling duck rise at once, only to be swept up in the net as soon as it was clear of the rushes.

We wove our way backwards and forwards through the marsh, along paths which were often, I afterwards discovered, parallel to each other and no more than ten yards apart. So little were the ducks affected by the passing of the boats that those ten yards away were left quite undisturbed. One part of the marsh seemed empty of ducks, and looking up into the bushes which in many places met overhead, I saw that the branches were full of dwarf cormorants. They were neat and handsome little birds with long tails, which they sometimes spread in a fan to balance themselves as they looked down into the glare of the light passing below.

When we emerged from the cormorant bushes the ducks seemed a little wilder than before. The *murdabchi* turned to me and pointed upwards. Above there was a great clear starlit patch in the sky. He shook his head and said 'Khoub neest', which means 'No good', and we headed back towards the hut. An overcast sky and complete darkness, I learned, is one of the essentials of duck-catching; rain is better still and snow is best of all.

During the half-hour we had been out just over twenty ducks had been caught. In the hut the wood fire was revived from its embers and we sat round waiting for the sky to cloud over so that we might set forth again. But after an hour the starlight was brighter than ever, so fitting ourselves like a jig-saw puzzle into the available part of the ten-foot-square floor (for the middle was occupied by the fire), the five of us lay down for the night. It was *not* a comfortable night so far as I was concerned, and when Mahmoud the gong-beater discovered that my leg made an excellent pillow, it became less comfortable still. But I occupied my time in thinking of the extraordinary things which I had seen and of their application to the catching of live ducks in other parts of the world.

I was determined to try and catch some myself and also to learn as much about the method and the significance of its various features as I possibly could. So I decided to stay on at Siah Derveshan.

CHAPTER SIXTEEN

MORE ABOUT THE CASPIAN SHORE

THERE followed several nights of clear starlight, and it was not possible to go out in the *murdab*. I spent the day with my clap-net trying to catch the greylag geese down on the 'pig-puddles'. They were the eastern pink-billed race, and quite different from our British greylag. But without decoys it was an impossible task. The geese were feeding over too large an area, and the 'pig-puddles' were too wet and bare to hide the sixteen yards of net successfully.

I spent four whole days in the attempt. On the first the net was set near the back of the bay, and I was able to lead the release wire to a tree at the edge of the wood. I climbed this tree and stood motionless in the shadow of the trunk, on a limb twenty feet from the ground. I stayed there from dawn until about midday. A white-tailed eagle settled once in the branches ten feet above me. I talked to him, but at first he could not locate the sound and was not at all alarmed by it. After several minutes, however, at last he saw me and flapped off in a great hurry. The bushes near-by were full of bramblings, shining brilliant orange in the morning sun. But the geese did not come near the net. They fed over on the far side of the bay, and in the afternoon Ayub and I moved the net. Ayub was the nephew of the *murdabchi,* a tall, handsome youth, and inordinately proud of the rubber waders which I had lent him. We conversed, chiefly by signs, and in the few key words which I knew, like 'here' and 'there' and 'this' and 'that', and we had the net set out in record time, ready for another attempt in the morning.

MORE ABOUT THE CASPIAN SHORE

The next three days, like the first, were cloudless, and the sky was brilliant blue. But the weather was cool even at midday, and very cold before the sun came up.

I had built myself a tiny hide of dead rushes and had roofed it in. To it ran the release wire of the net, and before dawn each day I would take up my position, and have my feet covered over with sticks and rushes by Ayub, who then retired to the edge of the wood. Each day I lay there from dawn until late in the afternoon, and arose stiff and disappointed but still hopeful of the next morning, when some new plan could be tried.

Walking out in the stillness before dawn the call of the waking Bewick's swans, who always roosted off the eastern point, was an additional help in direction finding; and when we were setting the net in the first grey light we sometimes saw an old boar go splashing back through the puddles towards the wood.

I would just have time to make sure by the pale daylight that the net was in order, take up my place in the hide and be covered up by Ayub, before the pintails and mallards came out from the *murdabs* inland. In great packs they would come tumbling from the sky to settle all round me on the pig-puddles. A little later the geese would come in from the lagoon, just as the snow mountains glowed with the unbelievable pink of the sunrise.

Throughout each day these greylags and whitefronts and mallards and pintails fed round my hide, sometimes within five yards of me, yet never would the greylags, which were my quarry, feed near enough to my net to be caught. Each day I tried a different method of concealing the net, and each day I was full of hope. At last one single bird stood within reach, or so it seemed, and I tugged at the trap-wire. But the pintails had dibbled about amongst the net so much, earlier in the day, that they had tangled it up. The net swung over slowly in soggy hanks instead of spread-out like gossamer, and the astonished greylag had plenty of time to fly out and make off with the rest of the army of wildfowl which had, so shortly before, been feeding peacefully around.

So ended my netting attempts on the pig-puddles, and that night a storm

GYRFALCON AFTER LESSER WHITEFRONTS *Oil Painting*

SMEWS ON A CASPIAN LAGOON *Oil Painting 30" × 20"*

blew up. The first of it was a strong warm wind out of a clear sky, and as I left the bay a great column of soaring pelicans swept along the shore. They were rising in a gigantic spiral without flapping their wings at all. As they swung round and round, some just starting from the lagoon, others already no more than specks in the sky, they shone brilliantly white in the afternoon sun, by reason of the pinkness of their plumage. Long after I had left the shore I could see them, a hundred strong, curling upwards on the thermal current which they had found, and which took them to so great a height without effort.

When darkness fell the storm clouds blew up, and it began to rain. At last I was able to go again to the *murdab*, and try my hand at wielding the duck net.

As before, we met in the little hut beside the log fire, where the smoke soon reduced me to tears. But after half an hour the gong was tied on to its forked stick, and we sallied forth into a thin drizzle. The *murdabchi* came to instruct me, and stood behind me as we pushed out along the narrow waterways. The scene was lit by the flickering flare, and the din of the gong filled our ears.

I stood, at first rather insecurely, behind the hood, holding the net ready. The boat was very tipply, and I did not feel very confident that I could wield the net at all and still retain my foothold. The eerie light, the fantastic noise, the thrill of coming, at any moment, upon a duck that would jump up just in front, produced such a feeling of suspense and excitement as I have seldom experienced. The whole thing was so strange and improbable, and yet here was I actually catching ducks myself in this unbelievable way. The ducks were very numerous that night, and almost as soon as we had started my attention was fully occupied. Teal slipped out from amongst the reeds, mallards jumped up with alarming suddenness. To co-ordinate the wielding of the net with the unexpected appearance of a duck looking bright and clear cut against the dim background of water and marsh, needed a high degree of concentration.

The hardest thing, I found, was to know when the birds that rose were really within reach. If they were not, and one made an unsuccessful stroke with the net on one side, that was always the moment chosen by a teal to rise quite close on the other. By the time one's balance was regained the teal was already out of reach.

I missed a great many ducks that I should have caught, but I managed to catch a few. One mallard duck swam against the side of the boat, and I was able to bend down and pick her up by hand, though I nearly capsized the boat in doing so. I scooped a white-eyed pochard out of the water, not perhaps with such a stylish stroke as it might have been, but none the less a successful one. I caught teal and gadwall and mallard and coot, and for every one that I caught I missed four that the *murdabchi* would have caught.

The drizzle seemed to make the ducks very loth to jump, and the teal had to be squeaked at in order to make them rise at all. Once I could have picked up a dabchick just in front of the boat, and later I tried to pick up another mallard duck by hand. She splashed so much in flapping along the surface of the water, however, that she extinguished the flare, and as soon as it was out, got up and flew away quacking loudly.

The boats were of primitive construction, and during the evening they leaked. It was practice, therefore, to stop occasionally to bale them out, and when we did so the gong-beater would usually take a short rest too. The instant that the gong stopped ringing near-by ducks began to rise, and in a few moments every one within fifty yards would be gone.

I noticed this, too, on later occasions, and I have no doubt that the gong plays an even more important part than I at first supposed. It is difficult to locate the noise, and almost impossible to judge how far away it is. Several times I thought that the second punt must have been left far behind, but, when I looked round, there it was, following close upon our stern. There is some subtle baffling quality about the combination of sounds, the clashing as of cymbals, and the deep ringing as of bells, which is bewildering to the ear of bird and man alike.

At the end of an hour I had myself caught a dozen ducks, and then I watched the *murdabchi* at work and learned much from watching.

LESSER WHITEFRONTS AGAINST THE PERSIAN MOUNTAINS *Oil Painting 30" × 20"*

CASPIAN PELICANS *Water Colour Drawing 4" × 7"*

On the following night again I went to the *murdab*, and since it was still raining, conditions were favourable to the catcher. In an hour he had netted sixty-five ducks, including shovelers, pintails, gadwall, teal and mallard. For February this was a fair bag, but I heard lurid tales of the dreadful destruction wrought amongst the ducks in the autumn when they first arrive from the north. My friend had that very season caught six hundred in one night, and across the river the *murdabchi* in Khinde Khale had caught over a thousand.

Yet the ducks seem able to cope with this drain upon their numbers, for I was told that no noticeable decrease in the duck population other than small annual fluctuations had been observed within the memory of the local duck catchers. Round the shores of the lagoon I myself saw such quantities of ducks as made it impossible to believe there could ever be a shortage. In one bay I estimated that forty-five thousand teal sat roosting on the soft mud. Elsewhere thick clouds of mallards rose from reedy marshes, and convinced me that the winter population of the lagoon was to be measured in millions rather than thousands.

Yet one must beware of being led astray by such mass concentrations of waterfowl, because for every one such centre that exists today there may well have been a dozen in past times. Ornithologists are agreed that wildfowl in North America have been more than decimated in the last century, and yet it is possible nowadays to see as many ducks in the air at once over one of the well preserved 'refuges' as it was probably ever possible to see anywhere, even in olden times.

Wildfowl *throughout the world* are in nearly, if not quite, as great need of the far-reaching and far-sighted protection which they are now enjoying in the United States and in Canada.

I was sorry to leave Siah Derveshan, where the catching of ducks was not solely a means of livelihood to my very hospitable host, but a highly skilled art in which he delighted to excel. In the ten days that I had spent there I had learned much of Persian rural life; I had learned the intricacies of a fish trap and how to take 6-lb. whitefish in it; I had learned that the art of throwing a cast net was not to be mastered in a day;

and most interesting of all, I had learned about the strange light which moves eerily through the Caspian swamps at night, lighting the reeds and branches with a mysterious glow, like Edward Lear's immortal "Dong with the Luminous Nose".

CHAPTER SEVENTEEN

FABULOUS BIRDS

'NOW *you'll* be able to tell me,' they always begin. 'The other day I saw a big bird. What would it have been? It had a white head and a black breast.'

'Of course,' I reply, 'it *might* have been a shelduck, only that has a black head and a white breast.'

'Well, now I come to think of it, that's just what this bird did have.'

There can be further developments on the theme. 'I'll tell you what, though,' say I, 'didn't it have rather a turned up beak?' 'That's right.' 'Well, I believe it was almost sure to have been an avocet, which is a very rare bird. How interesting!'

I have to be very brazen about this, because by this time I have little doubt that the bird in question was in fact none other than a magpie.

But sometimes the mystery bird is not so easy to identify. The most bewildering are those which are described by a reliable observer and which do not fit in with any known bird. I am left wondering whether my informant was mistaken or whether he has in truth discovered a species new to science.

Such a one was the 'Broon Brent' (my informant was a Scotsman). He knew the dark-bellied or black brent and he knew the light-bellied brent, and it was neither of these. He knew all the grey geese, and it was none of them. He lived in a part of the world where barnacles abound. He had even once seen a pair of rare red-breasted geese (on the Sabbath, and on the following day they had disappeared). But the broon brent was none of these, it was just . . . the broon brent. It was like a brent, but it was broon. In vain I pointed out that all brents are a little bit brown; in vain I explained that only *two* sub-species of brent geese are found in Europe, the pale-bellied and the black-bellied. 'I've shot yon broon brent here mony a time,' the old wild-fowler would affirm, and there was no shaking his faith in the bird.

I asked him to send me the next 'broon brent' he shot, and he promised he would; but I have never received it, though it is many years since he made the promise.

I fear the species must have become much rarer lately, possibly even extinct, and there appears to be no single specimen preserved.

The cream-coloured goose is another little-known species. It is figured in an old print which is one of a set of table mats. Its fellow prints depict such real birds as the thick-knee or Norfolk plover and the now extinct Esquimaux curlew. How the cream-coloured goose came to be one of their number is a mystery. It appears to be creamy yellow all over, with a pink bill and legs. Its nearest likeness in the realms of ornithology is perhaps the snow goose. But the snow goose is white and has black tips to its wings. On the whole, I incline to the theory that the cream-coloured goose is simply a near-albino domestic farmyard goose, and yet, *perhaps* in days of old there really was another species whose wing tips were *not* black, whose bill and legs *were* pink, and whose plumage *was* cream-coloured.

One of the most provocative species was the Russian duck. It all began at a petrol pump. From a gun and a couple of mallards in the back of the car, the conversation turned easily to ducks, and to an unusual pair which frequented a pond a few hundred yards away. They were 'rare Russian ducks'. The description was sketchy, and we were mystified. We walked over to the pond and there was nothing on it. The garage proprietor told us that they sometimes flew off, but that they were practically always there, and we went away still wondering what the rare Russian ducks could be.

Some days later we passed the place again, and decided to look at the pond on the chance of solving the mystery. As we approached we saw two enormous black and white ducks sitting on the far shore: they were farm-yard muscovy ducks. There the coarse old things sat, with a sheen of green on their wings. They awoke at our approach and the drake started waving

BRENTS AND A MACKEREL SKY *Oil Painting 30″ × 20″*

GREYLAGS COMING ON TO THE MERSE *Oil Painting 30" × 20"*

his head in the peculiar way that muscovies do, opening his bill, so that one might well expect a piercing call, but only managing to make a sort of puffing noise like some small steam engine.

The truly wild muscovy duck comes from Central and South America and is a bird of tropical swamps. It is black with a green sheen all over except for a white patch on its wings, and it is altogether more refined than its farmyard descendants. Few birds look more utterly bloated than an old domestic muscovy drake, with his bare red face puffed and swollen.

Besides 'Russian duck' it has many names—Barbary goose is perhaps the most attractive, or Brazilian goose. The name 'muscovy' is sometimes supposed to refer to the smell of musk which is perceptible in the plumage and also, they say, in the flesh of the bird; but another suggestion is that it was introduced into Europe in the latter half of the sixteenth century by an important firm of Turkey merchants styled the 'Muscovite Company', and in this connection it was even sometimes called 'Turkish duck'. Although it may have been first introduced at the time of the Spanish conquest of America, it was probably domesticated many centuries earlier.

But in spite of all these interesting associations with countries far from its native swamps, the muscovy duck remains one of the ugliest, if not *the* ugliest, of all water-fowl.

The Norwegian duck might have been a near relation to the Russian duck. We first heard of it from an old Lincolnshire wild-fowler, but he did not keep us so long in doubt. 'Some people calls 'em wigeon ducks for short,' he explained. 'Wigeon—Norwigeon, it's all the same!'

The golden goose, however, like the broon brent, has not so far been identified. It is said to be common in the Sudan, according to a friend of Michael's who was home on leave from those parts. Africa is a large continent and knowledge of its ornithology is not perhaps altogether complete, but so far only three geese are known to inhabit it; they are the great glossy black and white spurwinged goose, the dark brownish grey Abyssinian blue-winged goose, and the golden-brown Egyptian goose. The last of these was the most fancied for the title of African golden goose, but our friend knew it well and the golden goose was quite different; nor was it the same as the tiny and beautiful pigmy or painted goose, which is not really a goose at all, nor the knob-nosed goose or comb duck, which isn't a goose either.

What can it have been? Ah, what indeed!

On the Wash the wild-fowlers do not call brents 'geese'. They speak of them as 'crankers', which is a very appropriate name, because their call is well suggested by it.

A bean goose, caught in the nets, was brought alive to the lighthouse when I was away. He differed only from the pink feet, with which the local wild-fowlers are familiar, in having orange feet and legs and an orange instead of a pink band round his bill and also perhaps in being a little bit browner in plumage.

The fowler who brought him did not at once recognise him as a bean goose, but he was not to be caught without a name for him.

'What sort is it?' asked my man.

'Why, don't you know?'

'No.'

'Why that's a . . . a Scotch cranker, that is!'

I still have my Scotch cranker, and he is mated with a Hungarian cranker, a bean goose which I brought from the plains of the Hortobagy.

In Persia, too, I heard of a very strange bird. I was wandering on the marshy shore of a big lagoon, during my search for red-breasted geese on the Caspian Sea, when I met a fellow hunter. Instead of the usual muzzle-loading fowling-piece, resplendent in its polished brass rings and black inlaid stock shining with mother of pearl, he carried a breech-loading 16-bore. He spoke to me in excellent German, for it appeared that he had lived for more than three years in Germany. After discussing the birds of the district, and telling me of the rarity of red-breasted geese, except in very hard winters, he went on to describe the red-bellied duck. It was nearly as big as a goose, and of the goose-duck tribe, and it had a white head, a pale beak, black wings and back, and a red underside. They were to be found in pairs along that very marsh in springtime, but they were far from common, perhaps ten pairs on that twenty miles of lagoon. They were very tame, and one could walk up to within a few yards of them. He had shot one once, but

TUFTED DUCKS OVERHEAD *Oil Painting 18″ × 15″*

BLUE SKY AND SNOW GEESE *Oil Painting 30″ × 20″*

he did not shoot them any more and he was convinced that they bred there.

I could not guess at the time, and have no idea yet, what bird he could have meant. His description was so vivid and so sure, that, had we been in South America, I should have been inclined to believe that I was really listening to the description of a new bird.

Yet in one particular at least he must have been wrong. If he was wrong about the size, then he may have referred to the white-headed stifftail, a comic little diving duck which was to be seen out on the open lagoons in flocks, but which without glasses might well have gone unnoticed except in the breeding season. It is certainly not 'nearly as big as a goose'; on the contrary, it is a little smaller than a pochard, but the male does have a white head and a pale blue bill and a ruddy breast and belly. They are very tame too as a tribe, if one may judge from their American relative, the ruddy duck.

If he was wrong about the black back and the pale bill, then perhaps he meant a ruddy shelduck, which is chestnut-coloured all over except for a buff-coloured head and, in the female, a white face. The ruddy shelduck is my guess for the African golden goose, but it takes second place as a candidate for the title of Persian red-bellied duck.

'Wolf! Wolf!' is so often cried in the ornithological world that for years a real species was overlooked. This most romantic of all waterfowl is the Crested Shelduck.

Somewhere in Eastern Asia on a secluded lake amongst the great forests still may swim a pair of these magnificent birds. No one knows whether or not they are extinct.

The first known specimen of the Crested Shelduck was a female taken in 1877 in Korea, and it was believed to be a hybrid. It was clearly of the shelduck tribe but the crest was accounted for by the theory that one of its parents was a falcated duck, a beautiful Indian bird with a bronze-green head and crest.

No more Crested Shelducks were seen until 1913, when a pair were shot in Western Korea, and in 1916 another female was secured.

As soon as the black crowned head with the drooping crest, the delicate grey flanks, the black breast and the pink legs of the male and the striped head of the female were known, old prints and drawings were found in which they figured. Hitherto believed to have been figments of the artists' imagination, these pictures turned out to be accurate portrayals of the Crested Shelduck. So now *Pseudotadorna cristata* is recognised as no hybrid but the rarest of all species of waterfowl. It still remains, however, the mystery bird of the East.

THE CRESTED SHELDUCK, MYSTERY BIRD OF THE EAST

CURLEWS EARLY *Oil Painting 30″ × 20″*

CHAPTER EIGHTEEN

THE SHELDUCKS

MOST of the individual birds in this book have had names, but this story is about a pair of shelducks who shall be anonymous. This is not because there is anything in the story which I would hide, but rather because from what I know of their characters, it would be wholly inappropriate to give them anything so commonplace as a mere human word for a name.

Shelducks as a tribe lay their eggs in holes, usually disused rabbit holes, and since I have five pairs of tame shelducks at the lighthouse, I have built artificial rabbit holes in the bank for them to nest in, with concrete roofs and a slab like a paving stone over the nest itself, so that one can, on occasion, lift it away and look straight down into the nest.

One morning late in June, long after the normal shelduck nesting time, we discovered two eggs in one of the tunnels. This did not seem to be anything particularly unusual until on the following morning when we looked to see if she had laid another egg, the bird herself was on the nest. We hurriedly put down the lid again, but it was too much for her, and with a flurry out she came helter-skelter and away she flew. All the tame shelducks are pinioned and so we knew at once that this was a wild bird. She had chosen to make her nest in one of our artificial burrows, and of the half dozen vacant, she had chosen the very closest to the house, no more than ten yards from the garage door.

We were very worried, after our discovery, because we were afraid that she might have resented our intrusion so much that she would desert her two eggs. When next day there were still only two eggs in the hole we felt sure that this must have happened, as we had seen no sign of the duck herself. But it was wonderful how unobtrusive she could be, because on the day after that a beautiful clean cream-coloured third egg was in the nest.

We decided to risk no more and only to look again when we had actually seen her fly off, and for days we saw no sign of her at all. We never discovered when she came and went. So privily had she come originally, in fact, that before she flew off on that first day we had only seen her once, and that was more than a fortnight earlier when she had joined the pinioned birds and been involved in a deal of running and chasing.

It was some time later that we next saw her fly off, and this time she was joined by her drake, who accompanied her out across the marsh. She had eight eggs when we looked, but a minor tragedy occurred when a little sharp pebble fell down into the nest and cracked one of the eggs. It was only a tiny round dent, and had we had some 'new-skin' handy all might have been well; we tried a thick layer of oil paint but it was no use and the egg never hatched.

During the first part of her incubation the duck was rather shy, and if one talked loudly standing near the hole she was inclined to fly off. But later on she was too well settled to mind any amount of noise.

Quite near the entrance of the tunnel there is a small concrete pool and we thought that, if we ran some wire netting round this pool and the nest, there was just a chance that the old duck would stay with her ducklings and rear them. We put the wire round three sides of the nest, leaving the way to the entrance clear, because her habit when arriving was to settle down by the tidal pond and then run up to the nest. As the hatching date approached we saw more of her than before, and the drake often came with her, slipping out onto the marsh and settling there to watch over his mate from a distance of about three hundred yards.

When we thought that she had become quite used to the low wire netting we closed the pen all round the nest, so that when the young came out of the nest they would not be able to get out and she would either have to desert them or stay and brood them. There was also a danger that she would be too restless for them and exhaust them by running up and down the wire.

Against these contingencies I had a hen all ready which had been sitting for three weeks on china eggs. Should anything go wrong I could quickly

THE WIGEON ALIGHTING ON THE LEE SIDE OF THE LAKE *Oil Painting 18″ × 15″*

put the ducklings with the hen, which is one of the most usual ways of rearing young ducks.

On the morning after her nest was totally enclosed with the small mesh wire, the old duck went off at eight o'clock, and at four in the afternoon I saw her trying to get back to the nest. There were several people near and she did not quite dare to settle, but swung out again and joined the drake on the marsh. This was too long to have left her eggs when they were hatching, so we decided to look into the nest and feel if they were still well warm. If not there might still be time to save them by putting them under the hen at once.

When we lifted the lid there was a 'peeping' going on and I could see that the nest was full of ducklings, some of them already dry and fluffy. Three eggs were still unbroken. By next day still nothing had emerged from the hole and we decided to investigate again, as we had not seen the duck actually go back since the wire pen had stopped her from running to the nest. The mother was on the nest when we looked in and she flew off again at once. The three eggs were still unhatched and appeared all to be addled.

The old shelduck seemed so very wild that I was filled with doubts about our plan, and I decided then and there to take three ducklings away and put them under the hen, leaving the other two in the nest.

We kept an eye on the hole during the morning, as we thought; but two hours later, far out on the marsh, we saw the old duck running up and down the large mesh wire of the boundary fence, and behind her ran two tiny white balls of fluff. How she got them out of the little three foot high enclosure we never discovered, but it was certain that they would not long survive the dance she was leading them up and down the wire.

I was badly in need of young shelducks and did not want to waste an opportunity of rearing even a single pair, so we caught up the two ducklings and brought them back and put them under the hen. The old bird, who had flown off, returned with the drake and circled round calling, a sound so like a human laugh, and little suggesting her anxiety. She settled inside the pen and he with her: then they flew up and she settled outside and called again:

and then at once she decided that the ducklings were not there and she flew off far out towards the mudflats.

The baby ducklings started to feed that afternoon and took well to their foster-mother, who was now in a coop inside the little pen, and quite near the nesting tunnel. They were the most beautiful fluffy black and white things and whenever they got too far away from the coop they uttered most piercing 'peeps' which could be heard all over the lighthouse.

I awoke at about six o'clock on the following morning and I heard the calling of a sheldrake outside the window. I jumped up and looked out. On the gravel by the front door stood the drake whistling incessantly to his mate who was inside the little pen. Two of the ducklings had managed to get out of the coop, which had been shut up for the night, and were following their mother as she ran backwards and forwards along the wire. The drake stood very upright and occasionally ran a little way towards her. He had a noisy skirmish with a pair of ruddy shelducks and eventually drove them off. Then he ran back towards the little pen and his young ones, and stood waiting for his duck to bring them out. However she had got them out the day before, she evidently did not know how to do it now.

I went down to them, for the morning was cold and the ducklings should have been in shelter, either under their own or their foster mother. The old duck did not fly until I was a yard or two away, and then she fluttered down onto the edge of the sea pool, pretending that her wing was broken. A minute or two later she rose and flew round and her mate settled down by the pool. He too began to flutter around as if he were injured.

I decided that I should have to let them take away at least one young one, since they were evidently not tame enough to brood them in the pen, and since they would certainly upset the ducklings so much that the hen could not brood them either. By now, however, the ducklings had had such an adventurous introduction to life that I was not at all certain that they would survive if allowed to go off. At last I selected the largest duckling and let it out. Its mother came down on the bank and it ran directly to her. Meanwhile the drake was flying round, performing the most extraordinary evolutions. When he was about 20 yards away and almost overhead he would

TEAL IN SECLUSION *Oil Painting 25" × 30"*

WIGEON COURTING *Oil Painting 18″ × 15″*

suddenly bring his legs forward and come tumbling down as if he had been shot. Within a foot or two of the ground he would flatten out and fly round again, repeating the performance. This was undoubtedly a device to claim my attention and he did it fully a dozen times. Meanwhile his duck had led her duckling to the boundary fence. The duckling could easily get through it, but she did not think of flying over and letting it follow. So I walked down to her. She flew up when I came near and began to circle round, and the baby ran through. Near the river the drake was standing and the duckling ran down to him and sat by him, waiting for the duck to land again. He tried to lead it into the river and at first it swam out after him, but when the duck settled more than 50 yards away on the bank, it turned back and dashed ashore. She ran to meet it, and together they swam out to join the drake. There was a strong flood tide in the river, and I last saw them disappearing up stream in single file, the old duck in front, the old drake behind, and the little two-day old baby in the middle. I haven't seen them since.

* * * * *

The other four ducklings are doing well and growing very fast—faster, probably, than they would grow in the wild state. But in spite of that I am afraid that next year the old shelduck may choose a more secluded rabbit burrow for her nest.

CHAPTER NINETEEN

A PAIR OR TWO OF DUCKS

'WHY don't you try some ducks? They'd be nice for John when he comes out of hospital.'

'There isn't any pond.'

'We could make one.'

And so the ducks were started at Grantchester.

The lawn stretches for forty yards from the dining-room French window. At the far end we planned a semicircular pond with a radius of about seven feet, to be made of concrete. Behind the shrubberies would run five-foot wire netting and on the two paths would be gates.

It was all done quickly and when John came home there were two pairs of mallards and a pair of shelducks sitting on the lawn. Then the collection started to grow until now, just over a year later, there are nearly thirty birds there, of fourteen different kinds.

But that is not all. The most delightful part is the tameness of the birds. As soon as any one appears at the dining-room windows they all come rushing up the lawn. A little bowl of wheat lives on the sideboard and so a few kernels are always handy to throw to them, or to hold out to them, because they will almost all take food from one's hand. Usually there is an ugly rush and they clamber all over one's wrist and hand in a scramble to get the last grains which are wedged in between one's fingers.

There is a shoveler drake who is so confiding that whilst he is feeding from one hand he will step on to the other, and one may stand up with him whilst he goes on busily guzzling with his great ungainly bill. The shel-ducks will do this too, but they spend most of their time running round

A PAIR OF TEAL OVER FRITTON LAKE

Oil Painting 18″ × 15″

one's feet, from time to time trying the turn-up of one's trousers in case a grain or two of wheat might be hidden there.

The most showy are the Carolinas and the Mandarins. I am never quite sure which of these rather flashy drakes is the more beautiful and I still sometimes find it rather hard to tell their wives apart. Although they come from opposite sides of the world, one from America and the other from China, they are closely related. Of the Mandarin drake in full plumage one is tempted to say when looking at him, 'I don't believe it', and that is chiefly because of his extraordinary shape. His head with its flat sides seems to be made of wood and the fan-shaped chestnut feathers which meet over his back and stand up almost like two fishes' dorsal fins are unlike anything else in the whole duck tribe. A drake Mandarin is resplendent but he is also quaint, perhaps a little too quaint, and yet he is so oriental both in his quaintness and his splendour that he could only, in all the world, be a native of the Far East.

The Carolina drake is more duck-like in shape and his legs are *very* short, but his colours are deeper and richer, with the richness of dark velvet.

The Carolinas nested twice this year. The first clutch of eggs were all infertile, but the second clutch of six all hatched. The ducklings have the short legs and the long boat-shaped body of their kind from the very day they hatch. These ducklings grew very fast because they were rather spoiled. They had duckweed and chopped worms and a little minced meat to vary their diet of biscuit meal, and in spite of all the bad weather every one survived.

Then there is the wigeon family. The most handsome of them is undoubtedly the European wigeon, our own wild bird which comes in countless thousands to the coastal marshes in winter.

From the new world come the American wigeon and the chiloe wigeon. All three of these, in pairs, are at Grantchester. The chiloe wigeon comes from the southern part of South America, and the female looks like a slightly duller edition of the male. Like all ducks of the southern hemisphere, the drake chiloe has no eclipse plumage. He does not turn dull brown just after the breeding season, as nearly all the northern hemisphere drakes do. This brown plumage, which, for example, the European wigeon adopts in July and August, coincides with the moult, when, for a period, the bird cannot fly. So it has always been supposed that it is a form of protection to allow him to hide instead. Why the southern hemisphere ducks should not need this protection has never been explained, but the cinnamon teal, for instance, which inhabits both North and South America, goes into eclipse north but not south of the equator. There are cinnamon teal too at Grantchester. The drake is a glorious rich cinnamon red with blue-grey shoulders.

Another South American species is the rosybill, a diving duck who has forgotten how to dive. They are rather large for the little lawn but are so engagingly tame it is hard to replace them; I believe, all the same, that it would really be better to have some smaller and more decorative kind, such as a pair of Japanese teal or Bahama pintails.

The only other foreign kind of duck amongst the colourful crowd is the falcated duck who comes from India and Malay. The drake has a beautiful bronze-green head and drooping crest and the long mantle feathers of the back droop downwards too, with a strange weeping effect.

Then there are the English ducks, graceful pintails, comic tufted ducks, beautiful little garganey teal and quiet grey gadwall.

Such are the birds that live in the garden at Grantchester and never could I have believed that they would become in one year such an unqualified success.

To those who read this chapter and who may perhaps think that a pair or two of ducks would look nice in their own gardens, there is just one small piece of advice I would offer. Be sure that the very first pair of birds you have are really tame hand-reared ones. After that wild-caught birds may be added and they will soon become tame by associating with the nucleus of hand-reared birds. Ducks that come running to one's feet are so very much nicer than ducks that go rushing and flapping away as soon as one appears. If your ducks can live near enough to the house for them to see you constantly coming and going, and if, as you come and go, you sometimes have a grain or two of corn to distribute, they will repay you handsomely for your attentions by their tameness and confidence, and if they are really tame, few people could fail to find beauty and interest and sheer delight in a pair or two of ducks.

CHAPTER TWENTY

THE LIGHTHOUSE BIRDS

I WANT to write a chapter about the waterfowl which live on the salting at the lighthouse, and so I have brought my pencil and paper and a bucket of corn and have sat myself down on the bank to write it in their presence, so that they won't be offended and think that I am doing anything behind their backs.

When I came out of the door I called to them 'Come on', and immediately they answered me from away out on the marsh. There was a great babel of voices, led by the greylags and the emperor geese, with the snow geese joining in, and then as I sat down there was an ugly rush and a great flapping of wings as the geese came tearing towards me. They slowed up as they got closer, and walked up to me with an air of dignity, as though they were not hungry at all but simply chancing to walk that way.

Not so the eiders, who came waddling up and stood waiting in a little semicircle, pecking occasionally at the sleeve of my jersey. The eiders get their crops filled from my hand by what is nothing more nor less than blackmail. 'Until we are full', they say, 'we won't allow any other birds to come near you, so if you want the rest to come and feed out of your hand you must give us as much meal as we can eat first.' So the eiders are stuffed with meal, which they grab greedily from my fingers. Towards the end they become top heavy from the weight in their crops, and then they sit down and go on shovelling down what they are given. At last, replete, they wander off to drink, and to digest lying down, bulging under some tuft of grass. Then the more timid shelducks and the geese have a chance to come to my hand. In a collection of small ducks no one could describe shelducks as timid, but when they are amongst a crowd of geese their characters show up quite differently.

GARGANEYS IN SPRING

Oil Painting 30″ × 20″

THE LIGHTHOUSE BIRDS

The birds at the lighthouse have two special ways of giving me pleasure. The first is that they are very tame, and the second is that they attract the wild birds to come and live in the enclosure with them.

As I write there is a crowd of more than two hundred birds all gathered around me. There are twenty-five different kinds of geese from all parts of the world, and a great many different kinds of ducks too.

Two years ago it was impossible to see them at close quarters. Even a year ago they would go flapping away to the far side of the enclosure on impulse; but now with infinite patience we have at last made them tame. Many of them feed freely from the hands of strangers, and some of them will even follow me into the house.

In winter there are always wild wigeon in the tidal pools below the studio window. They come up to feed with the rest of the birds, keeping perhaps a little more to the outskirts of the throng; but to have a perfectly wild wigeon feeding within four or five yards is, to me, a thrilling event, and it is no less thrilling because it happens twice a day the whole winter through.

The wigeon have learned their tameness gradually. Only half a dozen come regularly to feed of the flock that fluctuates between a dozen and forty. But a pintail drake, which came for two days in the spring, had no time to become gradually tame. It was most exciting and interesting to watch him.

At the foot of the bank below the lighthouse, not more than ten yards from the studio window, is a sea pool, and on the bank itself at the edge of the pool is some long grass. In this grass my two pairs of pinioned pintails were wont to sit sleeping through the day, occasionally pushing out on to the pool to wash and then going ashore again to preen and afterwards to sleep some more. The visiting drake joined them and slept apparently as soundly as they, but when I emerged from the door at the top of the bank and called up the birds at feeding time, he was bewildered. At first he swam off onto the pool and hung about on the far side about twenty yards away. But as he saw his fellow pintails come racing up the bank to be fed, he did not know what to do. Very much on the alert he swam back across the pool and walked ashore at the foot of the bank. Slowly and with many a doubtful pause he began to climb towards me, where I stood with a friend by the door. He came up to within about four yards of us, and then stood, not far from the other four pintails, who were by now part of a great crowd of birds hurrying hither and thither after each grain of corn. He might have been thinking, 'How stupid those four are to go so close to those two human beings. Now, my mother always told me to keep well clear of them, as they were dangerous. I suppose they can't have been properly brought up. However, I feel it my duty to warn them. And see how they are eating all that corn. There's something very fishy about all this, something highly suspicious. I'll keep very much on my guard. Nobody's going to take *me* in. Oh no! Not *this* pintail!'

So he stood there on his guard. He never ate a single grain of wheat, but waited faithfully beside the others of his kind. Sometimes a duck scurrying from the peck of a goose would run into him and he would jump to one side and stand again alert and graceful, his long white neck stretched up, surveying in bewilderment the whole strange scene.

Two days later he had flown on on his northward migration and four pintails only remained at the lighthouse.

Of the geese that are clustering round me at this moment, undoubtedly the most beautiful are the little redbreasted geese. Their black and white and chestnut pattern, sharply divided and intricately interwoven, catches the eye at once.

At first I had two of them, a present from the Duchess of Bedford just before her last tragic flight. The redbreasts at Woburn Abbey, the only ones ever to have bred in captivity, lived there for fifteen years before they consented to nest. Now their offspring, hand-reared, breed freely every year.

These two turned out to be females and later I was lucky enough to acquire two beautiful ganders from a friend in Belgium. These four birds have now paired up and I am hopeful that next spring may see my first clutch of red-breasted goose's eggs.

Though quick to tame redbreasts have a nervous disposition. My Woburn birds will take corn from my hand, but only if my hand happens to be where they are passing. They will not come running for it as many of the

EMPERORS IN THE SUN *Oil Painting*

SNOW GEESE ON WET MUD *Oil Painting 30″ × 20″*

other kinds will. They are good-tempered little birds and their high clear disjointed double call is a cheerful noise to hear.

Lately the little flock of redbreasts at the lighthouse has grown because of some more which have arrived from Russia. But although I need no longer go to the North Caspian or to Siberia in order to have redbreasts feeding on the marsh at my home, I still hanker after the sight of a thousand of them in the air at once, and some day maybe I shall renew my search for these mysterious and elusive little birds.

Another beautiful, rare and rather mysterious goose is the emperor goose from Alaska and the Aleutian Islands. There are not many of these birds in the world, and the flocks, it is said, only migrate a short distance, for the south side of the islands is warmed by an ocean current from Japan and in winter the geese need go no farther south to avoid the snow and ice which covers their breeding grounds on the north side. Whether this is the reason for the emperor goose's short wings and bulky shape I cannot tell, but that they are birds of delightful disposition, very tame and gentle, strikingly handsome in plumage and most attractive in voice I do know, or so at least I have found the two pairs of emperors who but a minute or two ago were feeding from my hand.

Their merry chirruping call is always one of the first to greet me when I emerge at feeding time and they come to my hand eagerly for corn.

Fortunately there are few class distinctions amongst the lighthouse geese, though I have seen a certain amount of snobbery. The snow geese are usually to be found in company with the emperors, and on one occasion I heard a new arrival actually ask one of the lesser snows whether he would mind presenting him to the emperors. Of course, one can well understand that such a thing must make a great impression in the life of a wild pinkfoot—something to tell his grandchildren, but the matter has been a standing joke in court circles ever since.

My emperors, who were hand-reared, delighted in human companionship from their youth up and became much attached to the human voice. They travelled to the lighthouse in a hamper in the back of my car right across England, and they listened in silence to the music dispensed by the

B.B.C. through the medium of the wireless set in my car. But every time that the announcer's voice was heard, all four of them would call loudly in unison. Now that they are nearly three years old, when I hear their hum of conversation, like the soft baa-ing of lambs, close under the window, I lean out sometimes and call softly to them and I am sure of their clarion-clear reply, as they turn their white heads on one side to look up at me.

The most peculiar of all goose calls is made by that strange and slightly unbelievable bird the cereopsis goose of Tasmania. The cry of the female more closely resembles that of a pig than any bird call. It is a deep croaking grunt.

The cereopsis is a big bird and it stands high upon its legs which are pink, but it appears inadvertently to have stepped into some tar and to have emerged with its feet quite black. Its toes are less webbed than in most geese and the pads of its feet are more callous, which is said to be an adaptation for walking on hot lava in the volcanic regions it frequents. But alas, it has now become rare through overshooting and lack of protection. Its plumage is grey with peculiar black spots and its bill is pale yellowish green as its name implies.

The ganders are rather quarrelsome and I keep only a single female at the lighthouse and she is full winged. She often flies round the lighthouse on her great slow-beating owl-like wings, but she never attains any great height and she has shown no tendency to wander away. No doubt she considers the flight to Australia rather too ambitious a project, even in these days of aerial progress.

The swan goose, sometimes at the lighthouse affectionately called the 'Swoose', is a fine large bird which is rarely seen in captivity in Europe, though it is the wild form from which the farmyard Chinese goose was domesticated. It is a strange looking bird with a very long black bill, a long fawn-coloured neck with a chocolate stripe running down the back of it, and orange legs. But unlike its domestic cousin it has no knob on its forehead and its tummy clears the ground more easily. Indeed, it is quite a graceful bird, for as the trim greylag is to the farmyard goose, so is the 'swoose' to the Chinese goose.

PINKFEET LEAVING THE SHORE

Oil Painting 30″ × 20″

My pair of 'sweese' are delightfully tame and the gander will bury his great long bill in my hand with the utmost confidence, at the same time making his strange, deprecating, wheezy call and wearing a most disdainful expression.

I have quite a large flock of white-fronted geese whose calls bring back spring days in Hungary. That is where most of them came from, but one

is a young bird which with its mate frequented the lighthouse pen in the winter of 1936. They were stupidly shot near the pen one day and the goose was brought to me with a broken wing. She recovered and I have her still, but the gander was killed. Later in the same winter a single whitefront, also a young bird, with a badly broken leg came to the pen. The leg was dangling and she could not stand. She would feed lying down and then flap to a new patch of grass and start feeding there. I tried to catch her so that I could set the leg, but she was at first too wild. On the second day her mate arrived and from then on until the end of March they stayed at the lighthouse. By the time that they had grown really tame the broken leg had set itself, and though, if taken in time, I could have made a better job of the mend, yet in a fortnight she was able to hobble about quite well, and before she left she was walking strongly, if a little stiffly, on it with a pronounced limp. Whitefronts are not common near the lighthouse, and I was surprised that same spring when a family party of eight turned up. They only stayed one day, however, and were clearly passing through on migration. In the autumn of 1937 I looked in vain for the return of the lame goose and her mate. They never came; but four other whitefronts arrived in November, an old bird and three young ones. Soon after their arrival they took to wandering away onto the marsh, and one day when they were feeding just along the sea wall, a wildfowler came over the top, and only two of the four returned to the pen. They came straight from the scene of the tragedy and settled close by the lighthouse door, and from then until their departure in May they were wise enough never to stray. Occasionally they flew round, but seldom if ever did they settle outside the enclosure. They were two young birds, both females, and one of them attracted a pinioned gander, who was always with them. I do not expect them to return, for I believe that there is no regular migration route of whitefronts over the lighthouse. The ones that come are usually young ones that have strayed and got lost. But there is, nevertheless, just a chance that they might come back.

All these whitefronts have pinkish flesh-coloured bills, and their plumage is lightish grey-brown. When David first returned from West Greenland he brought with him a pair of whitefronts which had been hand-reared by the Eskimos, and whose bills were orange. Their plumage was much darker brown, almost chocolate-coloured. At first we thought this was just a chance variation, but two years later David returned to Greenland and sent home eight more whitefronts, and every one was chocolate-coloured, and every one had an orange-bill instead of the flesh-pink which is described in all the text-books. Four of these now live at the lighthouse, and the difference between them and the Hungarian and English ones seems more marked than ever.

Amongst the greylags on Brogden, the great goose marsh in Westmorland, a single young whitefront was shot last autumn. It was very dark, and it had an orange bill.

The questions which arise are: Where, if anywhere, are these dark white-fronts with orange bills common? Where do the ones which breed in West Greenland spend the winter? Not, it seems, in Eastern North America, for in that continent the whitefront is only known from the middle and west. When I have seen, as I hope soon to do, the white-fronted geese in California, including the giant whitefront or 'tule goose', which is said to be as large as a Canada goose, I shall know more of the subject.

In the meantime it seems that there is a western race of whitefronts, possibly wintering in Ireland, which is darker than the typical race of Europe and Asia, and has an orange bill; and this is analogous to the races of greylag goose. Our English and Scottish greylag, which still breeds in small numbers in Scotland and the Outer Isles, has an orange bill, and by comparison with the pink-billed Eastern race, is a much darker bird. It is clearly a very different bird, yet Alphéràky, author of the great Russian monograph on the geese, refused to admit in that magnificent work that there was or ever had been such a thing as a live greylag with an orange bill. When he read of such in English bird books he explained it away by saying that the description was from a dead bird, in which the flesh-pink must have turned orange when it dried up!

There are two pairs of these eastern greylags at the lighthouse to compare with our own western and, according to Alphéràky, 'non-existent' orange-billed ones.

There are strange nocturnal magpie geese from Australia, and tiny maned geese and ashy-headed geese from the Falkland Islands, barheads from India, bean geese and barnacles and brents, canadas and cackling geese. All these and many others help to make up a collection which gives great pleasure not only to me, but to hundreds of other people who come to look at them.

When I let the true collector's instinct take command, I think of the kinds which are *not* represented at the lighthouse and of the strange places I shall perhaps visit in search of them. Amongst the ducks there are many, but amongst the geese there are few. The rare Sandwich Island goose, which is too near extinction to be exported, and the kelp goose of Southern Chile, which dwells by the seashore and cannot live without the particular green seaweed upon which it feeds. Perhaps, some day, the Sandwich Island goose will become numerous, perhaps a substitute will be found for the Chilian kelp weed, and in the meantime there is always Korea and the mysterious crested shelduck.

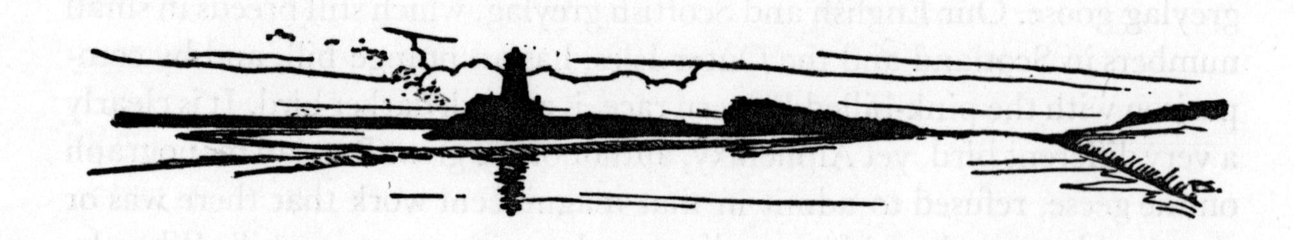

A POCHARD MARSH *Oil Painting 30″ × 20″*

BRENTS BELOW MOUNT STEWART *Oil Painting 30″ × 20″*

CHAPTER TWENTY-ONE

BEWARE!

IT is exactly one hundred years since the last great bustard walked the plains of England, but the species holds its own in other parts of the world. Such a loss, though sad enough, does not compare with the extinction of a species the world over. The tribe of wildfowl are not altogether immune, even in this age of scientific enlightenment, from such a fate. We may read indignantly of the great auk and the passenger pigeon and say complacently that such a thing could never happen nowadays, but only by the narrowest margin is the trumpeter swan of North America, the largest of all waterfowl, still included in the avifauna of the world. After a remarkable recovery there are now a few hundred individuals again, and it seems that the crisis is passed owing to the vigorous protection which it is receiving in its breeding haunts in Canada and its winter haunts in the United States.

Like the passenger pigeon and the Esquimaux curlew, the trumpeter has near allies which are still quite common. The whistling swan, though much smaller, is otherwise almost the same, just as the Hudsonian curlew closely resembles the Esquimaux curlew and the Carolina dove is but a smaller edition of the passenger pigeon. To scientists the loss is none the less on that account, but I mourn more the extinction of the little Labrador duck who filled a genus of his own and is now gone for ever. He was a sea duck akin to those romantic birds the eiders and his plumage was gaily piebald. Sixty years ago they were to be seen occasionally hanging in the markets of New York. No one knows why they disappeared, for they were little persecuted by mankind. We must beware that the rare spectacled eider does not share the fate of the Labrador duck.

The Hawaiian goose who lives in the Sandwich Islands is another species which has reached the danger mark. It is said that the introduction of the mongoose onto the islands is partly responsible.

CHAPTER TWENTY-TWO

THE MAGIC SPELL

IT is ten years now since I first fell under the spell of wild geese, and even now I am not quite sure what it is about them which still moves me so profoundly. But that there is something special about them I am not the only one to hold. Many people, like me, have become 'goose addicts', and the craving can only be satisfied out on the wild marshes at dawn, or dusk, or by moonlight. There is, I believe, no permanent cure for the habit, but then I have not met anyone who would wish to be cured.

On a morning in December 1928 I first watched great skeins of geese go inland to feed across a golden sunrise, and since then I have watched a thousand dawns. Yet every time that I see and hear the geese I feel again the thrill of that far-off morning on the Norfolk Coast.

I have seen at different times the massed battalions of a dozen different kinds of wild geese, but, to me, the chorus of the pinkfeet, first heard ten years ago, still remains the most glorious of all.

From the time that their music is heard over Scotland in late September, as they fly southward from their breeding grounds in Greenland, Spitzbergen and Iceland, until their return northward in April, the pinkfeet are with us, feeding by day on the saltings and in the fields, all winter through. At dusk they fly out to the mudflats of their chosen estuaries, their skeins tracing latticed patterns across the sunset sky. Under the moon the night is full of their wild cries, and on dark nights their calls come softly across the marsh as they move back from the edge of the incoming tide.

BY MOONLIGHT THE PINKFEET COME IN NEAR THE OLD TREE *Oil Painting 30″ × 20″*

PINKFEET HIGH UP *Oil Painting 24" × 24"*

They are our own pinkfeet, the wild geese of England and Scotland. Alaska may have its emperor geese, and Tasmania its *Cereopsis,* Hawaii its *Ne-nes,* and Chile its kelp geese. But we have our pinkfeet whose chorus is the wildest and finest of all, and I think, for me, their particular magic will never lose its potency.